The Dawning of Apostasy

A Brief Overview of Vatican II

The Dawning of Apostasy

A Brief Overview of Vatican II

David Martin

Published July 2013 by David Martin
Copyright © 2013 David Martin

David Martin
5815 E. Olympic Bl
Los Angeles CA 90022
jmj4today@att.net

2nd edition July 2013
ISBN: 978-0-9896429-34

"What was sacred for prior generations remains sacred and great for us as well"

— Pope Benedict XVI on the Latin Mass, April 30, 2011

Dedicated to
Saint Theresa of Lisieux

CONTENTS

This title constitutes the 2nd edition of our previous book on *Vatican II, A Historic Turning Point*, which aside from a new cover and some formatting revisions, has undergone no significant change.

We wish to extend our thanks to those individuals and organizations that contributed to this edition, especially Mary Rademacher for providing the use of her beautiful "Our Lady of the Roses Blue Book" which contributed significantly to some of the key graphic elements of this book.

We especially extend our heartfelt thanks to Benedict XVI and his successor, Pope Francis, for their untiring efforts to uphold the legacy of Faith which has been a *key* motivating factor in spurring this venture forward.

PREFACE

As God has established and guided His Church through the ages in the path of Holy Tradition, it stands that what He has established in the way of liturgical discipline must remain, as with the laying of bricks. For these disciplines "are adapted to all men of all times and all places." *(Pope Paul VI, Mysterium Fidei)* Any reforms that are enacted to advance the Church must always enhance and build on this same foundation as in the laying of new brick (e.g. St. Michael prayer after Mass), for therein is the hand of God adorning and decking his Spouse with new jewels that this same Spouse may shine forth with all the greater clarity and beauty for the sanctification of all.

But at the Second Vatican Council we saw another hand at work undoing the work of God under the guise of restoration, giving way to the structural collapse of the Holy City. In the words of Benedict XVI while still a cardinal: "What happened after the Council was something else entirely." What we have seen since the Council is not discipline but the unraveling of holy discipline. We have seen the molestation of Christ's Holy Spouse because the keepers of the Spouse handed her to strangers who in the name of ecumenism have abused her and stripped her of her jewels. Yea, we have seen the Holy City "half in ruins."

This mournful legacy had its beginning at the Second Vatican Council (1962-1965) which was the foundation of the liturgical reform. The general purpose of the Council was not to mandate or implement, but to propose, to draft, and to design. But in this new design the hand of God was not found because "a very powerful organization showed its hand at the Council, set up by the cardinals from those countries bordering the Rhine, complete with a well-organized secretariat." *(His Excellency Marcel Lefebvre, Open Letter to Confused Catholics, 1986)* This organization by nature was schismatic, and was the instrument of the adversary to divert the course of the Council right in the early stages.

With their control of the Council's drafting apparatus they were then able to draft up a new Liturgical Constitution to everyone's liking while camouflaging their true design to subvert the Faith. The game plan was to word everything ambiguously where the documents had a certain appearance of orthodoxy while at the same time proposing destructive changes to the Church.

The pope, of course, was never attempting to change the Church since his purpose for convoking the Council was to restate Holy Tradition as evidenced in his opening speech on October 11, 1962: "The major interest of the Ecumenical Council is this: that the sacred heritage of Christian truth be safeguarded and expounded with greater efficacy." *(John XXIII)* With dangers threatening the Faith, the pope wished to address certain key areas (e.g. birth control, evolution) where direct application was needed like a weed killer, but through the craft of the enemy the devil grass of modernism crept through the conciliar cracks and managed to strangle the attempted fruits of the Council. The pope's plan never surfaced.

There were outstanding and saintly participants at the Second Vatican Council who were willing and ready to assist Almighty God in the enacting of holy reform for the preserving of traditional teaching and practice. But according to Pope Paul VI their efforts were hampered by "the devil" who came along "to suffocate the fruits of the Ecumenical Council" so that the liberal reform prevailed. (June 29, 1972) The torch of Tradition was stifled and a new torch ignited which from that point would cast a false light upon the Church where, under the illusion of progress, clergy and laity together would degenerate into realms of darkness and apostasy unto the eventual abuse of one another.

This tragic debacle described is the gist of the Third Secret of Fatima which, because of its drastic content, was never unveiled. Unfortunately, it has had to reveal itself in action so that we may see with our own eyes what we have done to ourselves by our ungrateful attempts to bury the Secret. The Third Secret concerned this subversion of the Catholic hierarchy through which a wide body of the Church would be led astray.

But it didn't happen overnight. The post-conciliar revolution was foreshadowed in the writings of a nineteenth century Freemason and excommunicated priest, Canon Roca (1830-1893), who predicted that "the liturgy of the Roman Church will shortly undergo a transformation at an ecumenical council, which will restore to it the venerable simplicity of the golden age of the apostles in accordance with the dictates of conscience and modern civilization." He predicted a "new religion," a "new dogma," a "new ritual," a "new priesthood", and made known his Masonic aspirations "to deprive the Church of its supernatural character, to amalgamate it with the world, to interweave the denominations ecumenically instead of letting them run side by side as separate confessions, and thus to pave the way for a standard world religion in the centralized world state." *(Bishop Rudolph Graber PhD, Athanasius and the Church in our Time, 1974)*

Canon Roca speaks of a New World Order to come (Novus Ordo Seclorum). These false luminaries for centuries had anticipated the dawning of this false light upon humanity which would be the very antithesis of that true light emanating from the Holy Sacrifice that had led the way through the ages. The middle-late sixties was the dawning of this age of Antichrist wherein we saw this new wave reflected in our music and pop-culture, known by some as the New Age Movement.

But the Second Vatican Council was the major point of entry for this false light to enter upon the Christian community. For having penetrated the Church it was then able to inject itself into the veins of the Mystical Body so as to start engendering new thoughts, new affections, and a new formation for priests, religious, and laity. This false light known also as the *Spirit of the Council* was pushed through the Council by false luminaries like Fr. Karl Rahner, Cardinal Lienart, and Cardinal Suenens who would later become the head of the Charismatics.

Pope Paul VI lamented the outcome of the Council when he said: "The Church finds herself in an hour of anxiety, a disturbed period of self-criticism, or what would even be better called self-destruction. It is an interior revolution, acute and complicated, which nobody expected after the Council. It is almost as if the Church were attacking itself." (December 7, 1968 in his address at Lombard Seminary)

What follows is a brief overview of the Second Vatican Council and its turbulent aftermath. It shows forth in simple language how the Council was a historic turning point for the Church which led its people down the path of babel and confusion. The Church's mission from the beginning was to enlighten the world that it might be drawn to embrace Christianity, but with the Church today in eclipse both have tumbled together, fulfilling the prophecy of Our Lady at La Salette: "The Church will be in eclipse, the world will be in dismay." (1846)

But Deo Gratias, the Blessed Virgin today is lifting up Her heel in a final dramatic move to obliterate the forces of evil from our world. (Genesis 3:15) Our Lady calls upon the true apostles of the last days to go forward with St. Michael as their guide and restore the Church to its former glory. "For now is the time of all times, the end of all times." (La Salette) We are witnessing today the dawning of a great and glorious renewal for the Church as foretold in Holy Scripture: "At that time shall Michael rise up, the great prince, who standeth for the children of thy people." (Daniel 12:1)

St. Michael was removed from the Church's liturgy at Vatican II which opened the door to infiltration, but when he is returned this will open the way to a glorious restoration which will usher in the *Era of Peace* promised by Our Lady at Fatima. The cause of St. Michael assumes more importance today than in any period of history since he is the guardian of the Faith whose mission is to lead the armies of God in the last times.

We pray that the cause of Michael be returned to the Church and that traditional discipline be restored so that the *Church Militant* can again be girt with that brilliance and armor "wherewith it may be able to extinguish all the fiery darts of the most wicked one." (Ephesians 6:16)

David Martin

"A real change in the contemporary perception of the purpose of the Mass and the Eucharist will occur only when the table altars are removed and Mass is again celebrated at the high altar; when the purpose of the Mass is again seen as an act of adoration and glorification of God... and as the mystical reenactment of the Lord's sacrifice on the cross."

—Fr. Klaus Gamber, The Reform of the Roman Liturgy, 1993

"I will go in to the altar of God: to God who gives joy to my youth"

- Psalms 42: 4

A Historic Turning Point

In contemplating the sweeping liturgical reforms of the past forty years, it behooves us to take a second look at Vatican II and how it signaled a revolt from the everlasting ordinance of old. (2 Thessalonians 2:3)

From the earliest times the sacrifices to God were done facing the tabernacle, as seen in God's instruction to Moses: "Thou shalt present also the calf before the tabernacle... and shalt offer a burnt offering upon the altar." (Exodus 29:10, 13) The sacrifices of the Old Testament were a figure of Christ's Sacrifice that would continue perpetually in this manner through the priests, so that since the time of Christ there is no evidence of the Church having deviated from this pattern.

This point is affirmed by acclaimed liturgist Monsignor Klaus Gamber, whom Pope Benedict while a cardinal proclaimed as a prophet for our time: "We can say and convincingly demonstrate that neither in the Eastern nor the Western Church was there ever a celebration facing the people." Even from the time of Abel to the time of Pope Paul VI the sacrificial offering was always done facing God.

Vatican II marked [1]the first time in history that the priest offered the sacrifice facing the people with his back to the tabernacle (versus populum), fulfilling the prophecy that the continual sacrifice would be profaned. (Daniel 8:12) The dark forces

---

1   *The New Mass wasn't actually implemented until four years after the Council (1969) but it nonetheless was designed by the Council and is rightly called the Mass of Vatican II.*

entered the Church through the Council and engendered the reform of liturgy that has given way to an era of pacifism and religious indifference. Pope Paul VI would lament the outcome of the Council on June 29, 1972, when he said:

"From some [2]fissure the smoke of Satan entered into the temple of God" —Pope Paul VI, June 29, 1972

We might see Vatican II as the hatch through which the infernal enemy first slipped into the Church. The adversary knew that if he could get his foot in the door he could use the Church's liturgical apparatus to steer the Bark onto a new course if the liturgy were simply altered.

This is what happened at the Council. The 1964 conciliar instruction, Inter Oecumenici, article 91, called for "celebration facing the people" which diverted the Church from its path. The focus of the Council was now for "active participation by the faithful" around which everything was to revolve, as expressed in section 14 of the Concilium on the liturgy: "The full and active participation by all the people is the aim to be considered before all else." This new socialist ideal was most effectively spearheaded by the new liturgical celebration which set the stage for the new church of man.

The result has been spiritual disaster. Before the Council the Traditional Latin Mass that was said was like a powerful beacon that led the way through the centuries with generation after generation of sanctified fruits. But when they took away the old liturgical formula in the late 60s the Church lapsed into a spiritual eclipse that has since scattered the flock and warped their spiritual outlook, the reason being the New Mass

---

2   *The pope was speaking on the occasion of the ninth anniversary of his coronation. Later in his talk he said, "It is as if from some mysterious fissure, no, it is not mysterious, from some fissure the smoke of Satan entered the temple of God." The pope deliberately worded it this way to identify the fissure as something that is no mystery, namely, the Council.*

does not place Christ in center view before the Church; it was not the work of God.

It is for reason that St. Pope Pius V warned in his papal bull of July 14, 1570, (Quo Primum) that any efforts to alter the formula of the Mass as mandated by the Council of Trent would "incur the wrath of Almighty God and of the blessed Apostles Peter and Paul", since he already understood that any such efforts would be the work of heretics seeking to undermine the Faith.

Monsignor Gamber, whose work was highly praised by Cardinal Ratzinger (now Benedict XVI), had this to say about the change of liturgy: "The liturgical reform welcomed with so much idealism and hope by many priests and lay people alike has turned out to be a liturgical destruction of startling proportions, a debacle worsening with each passing year. Instead of the hoped-for renewal of the Church and of Catholic life, we are now witnessing a dismantling of the traditional values and piety on which our faith rests." (The Reform of the Roman Liturgy)

Cardinal Ratzinger himself had this to say: "What happened after the Council was something else entirely: in place of liturgy as the fruit of development came fabricated liturgy. We abandoned the organic, living process of growth and development over the centuries, and replaced it—as in a manufacturing process—with a fabrication, a banal on-the-spot product." (From his preface to The Reform of the Roman Liturgy)

Cardinal Ottaviani, who was special adviser to Pope Paul VI, refuted the New Mass in a letter to His Holiness on September 25, 1969, saying, "The Novus Ordo represents, both as a whole and in its details, a striking departure from the Catholic theology of the Mass." (From his cover letter to his famous *Ottaviani Intervention* on the New Mass)

The New Mass indeed marked not a renewal but a departure from the Traditional Latin Rite that had never changed through the centuries. Msgr. Gamber says that "unlike the appalling changes we are currently witnessing, the changes made in the Roman Missal over a period of almost 1400 years did not involve the rite itself. Rather, they were changes concerned only with the addition and enrichment of new feast days... and certain prayers."

The late Archbishop Lefebvre said: "To the new Mass there corresponds a new catechism, a new priesthood, new seminaries, new universities, the charismatic and pentecostal Church—all opposed to orthodoxy and to the age-old magisterium of the Church." (November 21, 1974, speaking to the seminarians at Econe)

A true renewal then is to go back to the pre-conciliar formula for saying the Mass, which is also the solution to the present crisis. "Today's Church has no need for a New Order of the Mass. What she needs is a flourishing spiritual life. This can overcome the crisis of faith, a crisis that is also a crisis of authority. At least in part, the responsibility for the crisis of authority must be squarely placed on Rome." *(Msgr. Gamber)*

A Brief History

The plan to destroy the Mass goes back many centuries and didn't just happen overnight. Luther, who founded the reformist movement, understood keenly that the way to destroy the Church is by destroying the Mass upon which the entire Church is built. "It is indeed upon the Mass as on a rock that the whole papal system is built, with its monasteries, its bishoprics, its collegiate churches, its altars, its ministries, its doctrine, i.e., with all its guts. All these cannot fail to crumble once their sacrilegious and abominable Mass falls." (Martin Luther, Against Henry, King of England, 1522, Werke, Vol. X, p. 220.)

The Council of Trent convened from 1545-1563 to condemn Luther and the Reformation and to mandate once and forever the formula for the Mass. The Council put the dog out as it were, so that reformers from that point were forced to operate outside the Church, barking at a distance, while the Church enjoyed that safeguard and liberty that came through the old liturgical formula.

But when they convened the Second Vatican Council the dog came back in. According to Michael Davies, virtually every prayer which the Protestant reformers removed from the Mass five centuries ago was removed during the liturgical revolution of Vatican II. It is no secret that six Protestant delegates were invited to the Council as consultants to advise the bishops in matters of liturgy and doctrine (see chapter 10). The reformist movement today is operating from within the Church and is using the Church as its stronghold against the Faith because the Council opened its doors and allowed secularists to come in and impose their ideas upon the Church.

John XXIII Innocent

Pope John XXIII 1958-1963

This of course was no fault of Pope John XXIII (morally speaking), since he convoked the Second Vatican Council in 1962 to defend the Church against the errors of evolution and modernism, and initially had presented the Council with 72 preparatory schemas that had Vatican liberals up in arms because of their strict and conservative agenda. Having read the Third Secret of Fatima, he was alerted to the powers of darkness that were encroaching upon the Church, so he saw this as an opportunity to restate the Faith. Though he was a bit naive, his objective was to rally the troops and use the Council to fight off the dark knights of secularism that were threatening the Faith.

But when the doors of the Council were opened the storm of conspiracy rushed in beyond his wildest nightmares. In an act unprecedented in Church history, the vote needed to determine the members of the conciliar drafting commissions was suddenly blocked when Cardinal Lienart, a Freemason, seized the microphone from the speaker and demanded that the slate of 168 candidates be discarded and that a new slate of candidates be drawn up. His uncanny gesture was heeded by the Council and the election was postponed. Lienart's action "deflected the course of the Council and made history." The date was October 13, 1962, the 45th Anniversary of Our Lady's last apparition at Fatima.

Note: This story of Cardinal Lienart and the coup is covered at length in Fr. Wiltgen's famous book, "The Rhine Flows into the Tiber" (TAN Books)

Council Hijacked

With the election that resumed, prominent arch-progressives and members of the Rhine group (so named because their countries bordered on the Rhine) rose up and captured the key positions of the Council, and were then able to scrap the pope's carefully prepared agenda which had taken over two years to formulate. Thereupon they quickly drafted their own agenda which in turn became the foundation of the Vatican II we know today. The Constitution on the Sacred Liturgy was adopted by the Council on December 7, 1962, which was principally the work of Msgr. Annibale Bugnini whom the pope had earlier removed from two posts because of sinister activity. The Constitution was in fact the outgrowth of the one preparatory schema (drafted by Bugnini) which Vatican liberals had spared because of its designs for a New Mass.

History indeed was made at the Council! What is mind boggling is the dictatorial force wherewith the conciliar elite took the law into their own hands and were able to junk the pope's outline for the Second Vatican Council (72 schemata) without a rebuttal. With the procedural rules laid down by the pope a mere one-third vote was needed to get the schemata passed, which in fact did pass by a 40% vote, but the Rhine fathers stirred up a sedition and insisted that this minority vote not be honored in favor of the 60% vote against the schemata, even telling the pope, "This is inadmissible!" They abhorred the orthodoxy of the preparatory outline with its strict formulations and resented the idea of having it imposed upon them by a pope who "clung to the old absolute traditions."

The pope, fearing a tumult, backed down and consented to let the Rhine fathers have their way against game rules. Though he had planned it differently, this was a failing on his part that marked a turning point in the Second Vatican Council. Hence, the most meticulous and painstaking preparation ever undertaken for any council of Church history was suddenly dumped to the gleeful consent of the Council majority. Only the liturgical schema remained.

Historic Coup d'etat at Vatican II

On October 13, 1962, Cardinal Achille Lienart of France deflected the course of the Council and made history when during a speech he seized the microphone and demanded that they halt the vote needed to determine the Council's leadership. His demand was acceded to and hailed a victory in the press, thus allowing the progressives of the Rhine coalition to rise up and capture the key positions of the Council. This then enabled them to scrap Pope John's plans for Vatican II and to draft up a new agenda of their own, thereby giving birth to the conciliar reform. Lienart reportedly confessed on his deathbed that he was a 30th degree Freemason, which would explain his illicit intervention. The preeminent Romano Amerio who had contributed significantly to the drafting of the original Vatican II outline cites how the legal framework of the Council was violated right from the onset: "This departure from the original plan" came about "by an act breaking the Council's legal framework" so that "the Council was self-created, atypical, and unforeseen." (Professor Romano Amerio, Iota Unum, 1985)

We gather that Cardinal Tisserant, the key draftsman of the 1962 Moscow-Vatican Treaty who presided at the opening session, was at the center of this coup to usurp the Vatican Council. According to Jean Guitton, the famous French academic, Tisserant had showed him a painting of himself and six others, and told him, "This picture is historic, or rather, symbolic. It shows the meeting we had before the opening of the Council when we decided to block the first session by refusing to accept the tyrannical rules laid down by John XXIII." (Vatican II in the Dock, 2003)

This story of what happened at Vatican II is well documented and has been told in great depth by Father Ralph Wiltgen, Michael Davies, Cardinal Heenan and others. Archbishop Lefebvre himself who was on the Central Preparatory Committee for checking and overseeing all the Council documents had this to say:

"From the very first days, the Council was besieged by the progressive forces. We experienced it, felt it. . . We had the impression that something abnormal was happening and this impression was rapidly confirmed; fifteen days after the opening session not one of the seventy-two schemas remained. All had been sent back, rejected, thrown into the waste-paper basket... The immense work that had been found accomplished was scrapped and the assembly found itself empty-handed, with nothing ready. What chairman of a board meeting, however small the company, would agree to carry on without an agenda and without documents? Yet that is how the Council commenced." (*Archbishop Lefebvre, Open Letter to Confused Catholics, 1986*)

The progressives indeed stormed the Council, though it was but a core group orchestrating the discord. It only took a few to get the fuse of revolution burning, but unfortunately many listened with itching ears so that in a short time the majority of the Council was burning in their flame. The conservative Bishop Adrian of Nashville relates: "As the council developed, some of the originally somnolent American bishops, catching fire from their alert European colleagues, became the able engineers of liberal proposals, going beyond the Europeans in ferocious, vituperative attacks on the Roman Curia."

Unfortunately, these European colleagues held the reins right from the beginning and were able to turn the Council fathers against Pope John's plan for Vatican II. The rejection of the 72 schemata had now opened the way for discussion of the one remaining schema on the liturgy which was quickly winning the applause of the Council.

It was then that Cardinal Ottaviani stood up and sounded the alarm at the Council, saying, "Are we seeking to stir up wonder, or perhaps scandal, among the Christian people, by introducing changes in so venerable a rite that has been approved for so many centuries and is now so familiar? The rite of Holy Mass should not be treated as if it were a piece of cloth to be refashioned according to the whim of each generation." *(Michael Davies, Pope John's Council, 1977)* Unfortunately, Ottaviani's words were brushed aside with derision and laughter. He was humiliated when they switched off the microphone during his speech, causing the elderly and half-blind cardinal to stumble back to his seat without assistance. It was this very spirit of mockery that gave birth to a reform that has caused the Church in our time to mock its own ancient traditions.

What is mystifying is why Pope John XXIII would even convoke a council seeing that his predecessors, Pius X, XI, and XII, had all refrained from calling an ecumenical council for fear it would provide a fissure for modernist infiltrators who were already plotting their entry. This truly was a mistake. Though he meant well and had the best of intentions, the calling of the Council was not the answer to fulfilling these intentions as he would later acknowledge.

The best he could have done was to release the Third Secret of Fatima in 1960, but he couldn't bring himself to do it because of the controversy it stirred among Vatican officials. They advised him against it and placed great pressure on him concerning this, yet he knew something needed to be done to restate the Dogma of Faith which, according to the Secret, was in danger of being lost. So he acted in good faith and did what he thought was right.

But in view of his decision to withhold the Third Secret in 1960, some had construed it as a slap in the face to Our Lady of Fatima when on October 11, 1962, during his opening speech at the Second Vatican Council, the pope said, "We must disagree with those prophets of doom, who are always forecasting disaster." Every indication is that his reading of the Third Secret is what actually prompted his convocation of the Council, as Cardinal Oddi seemed to indicate in his commentaries. But he didn't want people suspecting his motives since the Fatima Secret was scorned by Vatican bureaucrats for its dire and foreboding predictions. So in keeping with their likings he cast a slur on "gloom and doom" prophets just to throw the people off and break the Fatima connection, in keeping with Christ's stratagem, "Be ye therefore wise as serpents and simple as doves." (Matthew 10:16)

Pope John, too, is sometimes criticized for quietly lifting the ban on certain suspect theologians whose activities had been restricted by Pope Pius XII, but conservatives have faltered in not recognizing his good intentions. Monsignor Bandas, one of the true *periti* of the Council, had this to say: "No doubt good Pope John thought that these suspect theologians would rectify their ideas and perform a genuine service to the Church. But exactly the opposite happened. Supported by certain Rhine Council Fathers, and often acting in a manner positively boorish, they turned around and exclaimed: "Behold, we are named experts, our ideas stand approved."

Msgr. Bandas goes on to say: "When I entered my tribunal at the Council, on the first day of the fourth session, the first announcement, emanating from the Secretary of State, was the following: 'No more periti will be appointed.' But it was too late. The great confusion was underway. It was already apparent that neither Trent nor Vatican I nor any encyclical would be permitted to impede its advance."

Revelations From Switzerland Exorcisms

The following revelations are from a solemn exorcism that took place in Switzerland from 1975-1978 in which the demons under constraint were forced to reveal certain things about the Church. The session below is from June 18, 1977, and concerns John XXIII and the Second Vatican Council. Speaking through a possessed woman, the demons were forced by the Holy Virgin to tell the truth under the Solemn Church Exorcism, which was witnessed by several priests (listed below) who all expressed their conviction of the authenticity of the revelations made by the fallen spirits by the order of the Blessed Virgin. The exorcisms are recorded in a book by Jean Marty (translated from French by Nancy Knowles Smith) entitled, *Avertissements de l'Au'dela a l'Eglise Contemporaine - Aveux de l'Eufer.* The revelations have been edited slightly.

Exorcists: Abbot Albert-l`Arx, Niederbuchorten, Abbot Arnold Elig, Ramiswil, Abbot Ernest Fischer, Missionary, Gossau (St.-Gall), Rev. Father Pius Gervasi, O.S.B., Disentis, Abbot Karl Holdener, Ried, Rev. Father Gregoire Meyer,—Trimbach, Rev. Father Robert Rinderer, C.P.P.S., Auw, Abbot Louis Veillard, Cerneux-Pequignot. (Two other French priests also participated in the exorcisms.)

E = Exorcist
B = Beelzebub

E: In the name of the Most Blessed Virgin, tell us the truth!
B: John XXIII commenced his pontificate in 1958... He was pious and had good intentions, although things did not always turn out as he had foreseen. The fact remains that he convoked the Council, and he would have done better had he refrained

from doing so... With the Council, a very great mistake was made. Even today, he would be turning in his grave if he knew what its results are.

E: Doesn't he know?

B: Of course he knows. He already saw on his deathbed that it was not very smart. But it was already much too late. He did not know that this Council would have such deplorable, destructive, catastrophic, frightful consequences. He thought he was doing the right thing. He had good will. He believed that he was doing everything for the greatest good of the Church. He wished to renew what little needed renewing. Could he know that later, those cardinals, those fraudulent imitations of cardinals, those evil cardinals, would snatch the scepter from his hands and would plunge everything into this terrible state? Could he know that? He acted in good faith, so he reached Heaven. At all events, he is saved.

E: In the name of the Most Blessed Virgin, tell the truth and nothing but the truth!

B: He was humble and good, but he was not very gifted. At that time, it would have been necessary to install a very gifted Pope, knowing how to govern the Church and to maintain his authority in such a way that he could not be countermanded. But he learned that too late... He suffered bitterly for it on his deathbed, and he sent for some of his intimate friends, or those whom he thought were loyal to him. He told them that he would like to shout to the world: **"If only I had not convoked this Council!" Because he now saw the frightful consequences of it but was able to do nothing more...**

E: In the name, of the Most Blessed Virgin, tell the truth, and only what the Most Blessed Virgin wishes!

B: But those supposedly trustworthy men thought: "He is on his death-bed, he is no longer completely rational." When a Council has been convoked, one can't just simply say "We are stopping it" as if it were a tap which had been turned on full and only had to be turned off again. This Council no longer had a handle by which one could take control or slow it down. Things were already too far advanced for anyone to be able to do anything. The control was broken. It was already broken when John XXIII died. **Naturally, we [demons] were involved in the coup. We were trying to gain an advantage everywhere. Naturally, we did our utmost so that this tap could no longer be turned off to stop the flood. That is why you have dissensions which are deadly, catastrophic, frightful, and everything else the Devil knows how to create. His trustworthy men said: "He no longer knows very well what he is saying." The trustworthy men said to each other: "This must definitely not become known. Things are so far advanced, everything is so much under way and so involved, that one can no longer pull the foot out of the shoe."**

Pope John XXIII's reluctance in releasing the Third Secret of Fatima in 1960 must have caused him unspeakable sorrow for the rest of his life, for now he was witnessing the tragic fulfillment of the Fatima Secret. The very forces of hell marched into Rome in full regalia to take the Holy City captive, which was accomplished through the conciliar apparatus provided them by the rebellious Rhine fathers and their periti.

Meanwhile, the pope had now contracted cancer with only eight months to live, which greatly facilitated their plan to take control of the Council. With some sixty percent of the elective seats now occupied by the Rhine group, the Vatican II Council had been hijacked just days after its convocation on October 11, 1962. As Fr. Wiltgen says in his famous book, "The Rhine had begun to flow into the Tiber."

The Concilium

What ultimately ensued were sixteen conciliar documents of distorted constitution, the most significant of these being the document on the sacred liturgy issued December 4, 1963, *Sacrosanctum Concilium,* which proposed changes to the Mass. The document did not actually mandate some of the drastic reforms later implemented but it nonetheless proposed them (e.g. use of vernacular) and called for an overall revision of the Mass wherein archaic "elements" accumulated through time "are now to be discarded" and "the rites are to be simplified" so that "active participation by the faithful may be more easily achieved." [article 50]

The document also said that "other elements which have suffered injury through accidents of history are now to be restored." [50] This would include the injury suffered by Luther and the Reformation through their expulsion by the Council of Trent, which Vatican II lamented as an unfortunate "accident of history." Elements of Protestantism indeed were "restored" after the Council to desacralize the Mass so that we would see the Mass as an assembly or community gathering where the common people perform the liturgical prayers. Take for instance article 53 of the Concilium:

"On Sundays and feasts of obligation there is to be restored, after the Gospel and the homily, "the common prayer" or "the prayer of the faithful." By this prayer, in which the people are to take part, intercession will be made for holy Church, and for the civil authorities."

In the centuries prior to the Council there never existed a "common prayer" in the Roman Rite, yet Vatican II calls for a "restoration" of this as if it had been lost. The common prayer in fact is a protestant practice stemming from the Reformation, and is among those elements which "suffered injury through accidents of history" which were now being "restored." The plan of the Council was to reinstate these elements under the pretext of a renewal in order to justify it before the faithful. With this same pretext they proceeded to change the Liturgy, as we see in article 21 of the Concilium:

"Holy Mother Church desires to undertake with great care a general restoration of the liturgy itself. For the liturgy is made up of immutable elements divinely instituted, and

of elements subject to change. These not only may but ought to be changed with the passage of time."

Not so! The old rite of the Mass is the inspired, immutable work of God that may never be changed by dissatisfied man. It was divinely engendered and guided through the ages in all its detail and needed no restoring in 1962. This quest for restoration accuses Holy Tradition of having been deficient, as we read in this same section:

"In this restoration, both texts and rites should be drawn up so that they express more clearly the holy things which they signify; the Christian people, so far as possible, should be enabled to understand them with ease [vernacular] and to take part in them fully, actively, and as befits a community." [21]

Here the document apologizes for the Traditional Rite, and tempts the faithful by proposing a new and easy format which caters to their basic, fallen nature of wanting things their way. And too, it accuses the old Mass of having alienated them, thus causing them to turn against their own spiritual heritage.

Yet, the document feigns fidelity to Tradition. Throughout the Concilium the claim is made that uniformity and traditional discipline should remain intact, whereupon in the very next paragraph or chapter proposals are made to the contrary. Consider the apparent discipline and uniformity proposed in article 23:

"Notable differences between the rites used in adjacent regions must be carefully avoided."

Compare now to article 37:

"In the liturgy, the Church has no wish to impose a rigid uniformity [old Mass]... rather does she respect the genius and talents of the various races and peoples. Anything

in these peoples' way of life which is not indissolubly bound up with superstition and error she studies with sympathy... Sometimes in fact she admits such things into the liturgy itself."

Here the Council invites cultural diversity into the liturgy. The ordinance and genius of the Omnipotent One is cast aside for the so-called genius of races and peoples who neither are capable nor authorized to introduce elements of worship into the Church. Contradictions and denials of this sort are not difficult to find in the Council documents. Note the false allegiance to the Council of Trent in the following verse:

"The dogmatic principles which were laid down by the Council of Trent remaining intact, communion under both kinds may be granted when the bishops think fit, not only to clerics and religious, but also to the laity." [Concilium 55]

The Council of Trent decreed:

"Laymen and priests not celebrating are to communicate under the one species of bread only... under no circumstances is the use of the chalice to be permitted to anyone." [18]

Herein we see violated the decree of Trent as well as "the dogmatic principles which were laid down by the Council" since receiving under two kinds fosters the heretical notion that the consecrated Host is the Body of Christ only and that the consecrated Wine is the Precious Blood only, and that the reception of both therefore is necessary for a valid Communion. However the Council of Trent decrees:

"If anyone denies that in the venerable sacrament of the Eucharist the whole Christ is contained under each form and under every part of each form when separated, let him be anathema." [Canon III]

By receiving Communion under two kinds the faithful are actually receiving Communion twice. Receiving under two forms also assists the reformist plan to treat the Eucharist as a symbol of Christ's Body and Blood since the symbolic connection is made much easier with the two species (bread and wine) than with one. And too, it encourages the idea of the Mass being a community meal and gathering, which was the view of reformers in Luther's time. These and other like ideas have resurfaced in our time through the Concilium which called for a *Restoration of the Liturgy* in the first chapter. This opening section laid the theological groundwork in order to justify their projected 'renewal' of the liturgy.

But what were they renewing but elements of protest that the Church had already condemned! There was no restoration needed in 1962, since the liturgy was already in perfect shape. Perhaps it could be said that a slight modernist dust had begun to settle onto the Church at that time which could have used a little wiping off. Perhaps it could be said that there were some liturgical screws that were starting to come loose in our practice that needed a little tightening up. But there was nothing of the Church's Constitution that needed renewing or updating in 1962, as neither did the Scriptures.

What needed renewing was the faith of the clergy which had grown somewhat stale at that point, thus rendering them vulnerable to change. The bishops simply needed to renew their allegiance to the everlasting decree of Trent which was one of the objectives of John XXIII at the Vatican Council. Had the Council gone according to his plan it may have turned out to be one of the great councils of Church history, but unfortunately the scepter was taken from his hands by progressive innovators, thus opening the door to an era of innovation and change. The end result has been a spiritual wasteland with virtually every diocese and parish going in its own direction today. It seems the New Order of confusion is the one common denominator that ties them together.

With Vatican II we have gone from revering the everlasting ordinance to having a do-it-yourself liturgy. One of the most ridiculing elements of the New Liturgy is its makeshift, snap-together design where the faithful are given multiple options to choose from, whether it be Eucharistic Prayer no's 1, 2, 3 and 4, or this or that acclamation or proclamation, etc. Introducing accessory parts to the Mass was deliberately done to encourage a sense of creativity where clergy and laity could freely "express themselves" in whimsical fashion. This is confirmed by Bugnini's own rationale for introducing options to the Mass: "The greatest liberty was given to choose between the various formulas, to individual creativity." (July 2, 1967, concerning the Second Instruction on Vatican II)

Active Participation

At the heart of the Concilium is its central theme of "active participation by the faithful" as expressed in article 14: "Mother Church earnestly desires that all the faithful should be led to that full, conscious, and active participation in liturgical celebrations which is demanded by the very nature of the liturgy, and to which the Christian people, *'a chosen race, a royal priesthood, a holy nation, a redeemed people' (1 Peter 2:9)* have a right and obligation by reason of their [3]baptism."

Here conciliar draftsmen have put their own twist on the scripture to enhance their own revolutionary designs. The scriptural verse about "a royal priesthood" is merely figurative to indicate the sacrificial nature of the Church since the principal function of a priest is to offer sacrifice, so in that sense we are a sacrificial or priestly people. We are called to atone and to follow the sacrificial Lamb in His sacrificial sufferings

---

3   *Note how baptism is used here as a pitch for human rights. Our baptism indeed calls us to go into the Lord's vineyard and witness for the Faith as Catholic militants, but it does not call us to go into the Lord's office and try to be "a royal priesthood."*

that we might reign with Christ as "a royal priesthood, a holy nation." This verse references our call to atonement and has nothing to do with the priestly office and its functions as the document deceptively implies.

This is an insidious attack on the priesthood where the people are instigated to compete with the priests and assume their functions as if they were priests. It calls to mind the sedition of Core and his men who demanded that they be allowed to perform the priestly functions of the sanctuary for which God utterly destroyed them. (Numbers 16:31) It in fact is the foundation of this latter day revolution wherein the laity have completely overrun the priesthood through the rampant use of Eucharistic ministers, lay presiders, women lectors and the like. It was Lenin who advocated the "empowerment of the people" and it was his disciples who sat in on Vatican II.

Priesthood Attacked

What we see today is a new socialistic church that is "for the people and by the people." With the Council came the new definition of priesthood as *The people of God.* It sees the whole Church as one hierarchy or priesthood but in different ranks, with the ordained ministerial priesthood being only one rank of this priesthood. "The people of God is not only an assembly of various peoples, but in itself is made up of different ranks." [LG 13] What is promoted here is the fallacy that we are all priests of one hierarchy.

"The common priesthood of the faithful and the ministerial priesthood are nonetheless ordered one to another; each in its own proper way shares in the one priesthood of Christ." [Lumen Gentium 10]

For the record, there is no such thing as a "common priesthood of the faithful." This was Luther's idea. The priest alone offers the Holy Sacrifice, and there is nothing the laity could possibly do to offer this Sacrifice, nor can they contribute to it in any degree for the simple reason that they are not empowered; they have not been anointed by the Holy Spirit. The best they can do is to offer for their intentions what has been provided them by the priest (the Mass), but the priest alone says the Mass because he alone represents Christ as the *Alter Christus* through whom the Holy Sacrifice is offered.

Naturally, it is Jesus Christ who offers the Eternal Sacrifice since He alone mediates between Heaven and earth, but he does this through His representative, the priest, who at the Consecration is as Christ saying the Mass. The priest is merely a place holder who stands in Christ's stead during the Sacrifice, and only the priest can fulfill this role with no help or contribution from anyone else since no one else is empowered to execute the functions of the priesthood.

Unfortunately the democratic principles introduced at the Council have greatly diminished the role of the priest where he is now seen as nothing more than the "president of an assembly" after the manner of protestants. The idea of appeasing God through the Holy Sacrifice has virtually been replaced with appeasing the people with change. The constant fuss today about "Scripture" and "Liturgy of the Word" was deliberately introduced to take away from the Mass and to plug the protestant idea of "Bible only." The constant harping on pet terms and clichés foreign to the Church's vocabulary (e.g. People of God, ministry, reconciliation, [4]initiation, renewal, etc.) should have been a clear signal to the faithful that a new program of indoctrination was underway. The clamor circulated at the Council about human rights, human dignity and religious liberty worked together to nourish this tumor of intellectual pride so that the Church in our time is now infected with its cancer.

---

4   *This whole language of initiation is the language of the Freemasons who themselves are secret society initiates. Through their influence the Rite of Christian Initiation (RCIA) was set up to reform Catholic thinking so that we would see baptism as an initiation into a community or brotherhood.*

Vatican II Not Misinterpreted

Vatican II certainly was not misinterpreted as some think but has been interpreted according to plan. A major concern of reformers even before the Council was how Vatican II would be implemented after the Council, so with this in mind the documents were worded [5]ambiguously where proposals often had a double or multiple meaning that would lend itself to their plan later when they could just interpret it their own way. These wordings were like time-bombs inserted in the documents set to go off later. The conservatism suggested by some of the wordings was only a smokescreen to conceal their true design to implement liberally as proposed in the same wordings.

For instance, in article 7 of the Concilium it states: "In the liturgy the whole public worship is performed by the Mystical Body of Jesus Christ, that is, by the Head and His members." On the surface this sounds very holy, that we are all called to adore God at Mass with one mind, which indeed we are. But what they really mean is that the lay people perform the liturgy, not just the priest, and that they too assume duties and dignities of the priest as part of a "common priesthood" as if they collectively were the priest through whom Christ works. It in fact advocates a spirit of revolution against the priesthood in keeping with the Council's theme of human rights (see chapter 9).

This ties in with the often repeated theme of "active participation by the faithful" which is another ambiguous bombshell. On the surface this perhaps can be taken to mean that Catholics should actively be involved with their religion by reading the lives of the saints, going to confession and sanctifying their

---

5   *The ambiguities were woven into the documents by a coterie of renowned Modernist theologians, including Cheno, Kung, Schillebeeckx, Fring, Danielou, Rahner, de Lubac, and others whose teachings had been condemned or censured under Pius XII. They in turn were assisted by a number of non-Catholics attending the Council. (Michael Davies, Pope John's Council)*

souls in the fear of God. But what they really mean is that they should be busy-body activists engaging in the liturgical revolution against the priesthood. Though the particulars of today's revolution are not necessarily mentioned in the Council documents (e.g. lay lectors, Eucharistic ministers), they nonetheless have their foundation in the documents and fulfill the Vatican II vision of "active participation by the faithful."

Picnic Outdoor Mass with Woman Lector

If the documents had been worded too bluntly it would have looked too conspicuous and alarming and may not have elicited the needed signatures at the end of the Council, so they just low-balled it a bit and obscured the lines in such a way where it perfectly lent itself to their plan. The wording of all sixteen documents was deliberately planned this way where proposals have an ambiguous or double meaning which can be interpreted more than one way.

For instance, the term "religious communities" which normally would mean Catholic communities is often used in the documents to mean non-Catholic communities, or the word "catholicity" which normally would mean our oneness with the Church of Rome is now used to mean oneness with the universal body of world churches. The end result of this double-talk is that union with Christ has been diminished while unity with the world has been enhanced.

Christo Centric vs. Ego Centric

In every which way the Vatican II Council undermines the Christo-centric concept of the Eucharist as opposed to the old Tridentine formula which so beautifully nurtured it through the centuries. This is seen in the second chapter of *Institutio Generalis* which sets forth a new and humanistic definition of the Mass never before seen in Church history:

"The Lord's Supper or Mass is a sacred meeting or assembly of the people of God, met together under the presidency of the priest, to celebrate the memorial of the Lord. Thus the promise of Christ applies eminently to such a local gathering of holy Church: "Where two or three are gathered together in My name, there am I in their midst" (Mt. XVIII, 20).

Here we see the Mass reduced to a meeting or assembly in which Christ's sacrifice is merely remembered. There is no reference made whatsoever to the reenactment of Christ's sacrifice which is the very essence of the Mass and the very center of all Christian worship. The miracle of Transubstantiation alone is what brings about the physical and supernatural presence of Christ at Mass, yet the document heretically implies that His presence is brought about by the assembly of people numbering two or more, as if they collectively were the priest. The gathering of two or more has absolutely nothing to do with the Mass, nor is their presence necessary for a valid Mass. This is a protestant idea which underscores the new post-conciliar church of man, which is ego-centric and not Christo-centric.

Christo-centric means keeping oneself out of the picture and forgetting one's surroundings and thinking only of Christ on the cross. It means renouncing the friendship of the world and seeking only the friendship of Christ, remembering that "Whosoever therefore will be a friend of this world, becomes an enemy of God." (James 4:4) It means dying to all things as taught by the Savior: "Unless the grain of wheat falling into the ground die, it remains alone. But if it die, it brings forth much fruit. He that loves his life shall lose it; and he that hates his life in this world, keeps it unto eternal life." (John 12: 24, 25)

Through the institution of the Mass Christ planted His death in our midst (1 Corinthians 11:26) that we too might follow His lead. Through our baptism we take on the robes of the Passion and walk the road of mortification, and why? Because we are members of His Body and we are called to join with Him. That is, we die with Him—we die to self and sin, we die to the elements of the world. **It is in this manner that the faithful are called to have active participation in the Sacred Mysteries.**

The Mass summons us to participate in Christ's sacrifice and to meditate on His death. Through the Mass Christ draws us into union with His own sufferings, that through these sufferings we might be purified and made one with Him. This union automatically puts us in union with the other members of Christ throughout the world without having to be sensibly aware of their presence, the reason being it is a spiritual union and not an earthly one.

In other words, our union with the other members of Christ has nothing to do with human encounter or turning to one another and saying "peace be with you." Nor does such encounter put us in touch with Christ. Modernists would have us think that we are the literal components of Christ's Body so that by turning to one another we are turning to God. This fulfills the prophecy of the future Pius XII in 1931 when he said that the church soon "will be tempted to believe that man has become God."

Let us not forget that the membership of the Church is properly called the *Mystical Body of Christ,* not the Body of Christ. The Body of Christ refers to the Holy Eucharist which is the True Body, and the Mystical Body must revolve around this True Body. But innovators today have put their own twist on 1 Corinthians 12 to condition the faithful with a form of human guru worship that would have them think they are the components of the True Body, even telling them that they are "the Eucharist." Accordingly, communicants in some parishes even respond "we are" when receiving Communion. Through insidious indoctrination (RCIA) the ancient serpent today is working to instill his own dispositions of pride into the church, since his plan is to build an activist movement where the people believe they're empowered by the Spirit to run about and dismantle the Church in the name of *Renew.*

What is needed is a true renewal where the light of tradition can again shine through the liturgy and dispel the present darkness. The design of the Eternal Master was to set this light upon a candlestick and raise it up before the world that it might illuminate the nations and attract all to the eternal riches of Christ. As He says, "A city seated on a mountain cannot be hid. Neither do men light a candle and put it under a bushel, but upon a candlestick, that it may shine to all." (Matthew 5: 14, 15) In like manner, the Traditional Mass must be held up high in every cathedral and parish of Christendom and not buried in local hospital chapels or hideouts lest we discriminate against the goodness of God.

Christ gave us his Church that it might be a light to the nations signified by the Latin word, *Lumen Gentium.* The light of Tradition emanating from the Old Rite is that *Lumen Gentium* wherewith to attract the world to Christ, but by withholding this light from the world the Church in our time is hindering the plan for man's salvation. What Our Lady prophesied at La Salette has truly come to pass: "The Church will be in eclipse, the world will be in dismay." (1846)

Pope Paul VI

Following the death of John XXIII on June 3, 1963, came the election of Pope Paul VI who is generally credited as the author of the New Mass. It should be noted, however, that he did not initiate or design the New Mass. The authors of the New Liturgy only promulgated it in his name to give it credibility before the Church, but he himself was not the architect, nor did he author the December 4, 1963 Concilium which bears his name.

Pope Paul VI 1963-1978

On February 29, 1964, the pope appointed Msgr. Bugnini to head the new Vatican II Consilium for the implementation of the Constitution on Sacred Liturgy, apparently not knowing that he had been dismissed earlier by John XXIII. With their sphere of influence the Bugnini cabal had managed to keep the matter low key, knowing they were to confer later with the new pope about getting him reinstated. Hence the pope naively complied with their plan trusting that Bugnini would carry out his commission in good faith.

But during the course of the Council the pope grew increasingly disturbed at discussions circulating about new formulas for the Mass. Though he initially had reposed hope in the reform, even contributing somewhat, he was never attempting to breach Tradition or invent a New Mass and did not agree with these new formulas being proposed. Eventually he would wash his hands of the liturgical reform and uphold the Mass of the Council of Trent in his encyclical of September 3, 1965, entitled Mysterium Fidei.

The point of the encyclical was to bring into focus the sublime mystery of the Holy Eucharist as the center-piece of our Faith and how the Church may never resort to flippant or careless wording in proposing such mysteries lest we give rise to irreverent and scandalous notions concerning the Holy Sacrifice *(e.g. the Eucharist is holy bread, the Mass is a meal, the Mass is a community gathering, the Mass is a celebration, etc.)* With this premise being established, he goes on to say:

"The Church, therefore, with the long labor of centuries and the help from the Holy Ghost has established a rule of language [Tridentine Liturgy], confirming it with the authority of the Councils. This rule which has often been the watchword and banner of orthodox Faith must be religiously preserved... Let no one presume to change it at his own pleasure or under the pretext of new knowledge. Who would ever tolerate that the dogmatic formulas used by the ecumenical councils for the mysteries of the Holy Trinity and the Incarnation be judged as no longer appropriate for men of our times and therefore that other formulas be rashly substituted for them? In the same way, it cannot be tolerated that any individual should on his own authority modify the formulas used by the Council of Trent to propose the Eucharistic Mystery for our belief... These formulas are adapted to all men of all times and all places."

Old Mass Never Abrogated

Though it is not common knowledge, it was determined in 1986 by a panel of nine cardinals from the Curia that Pope Paul VI never abrogated the Mass of Pius V, nor did he mandate the New Mass, nor did he ever grant bishops the right to forbid or restrict priests from saying the Tridentine Latin Mass. The Mass of Pius V remains in force to this day according to their finding. Pope John Paul II had commissioned the cardinals to look into the legal status of the old Mass as it was his intention to bring its legality to light.

This in turn laid the groundwork for Benedict XVI to continue the process of liberating the old rite when he issued his Moto Proprio on the Latin Mass on July 7, 2007, reaffirming the legality of the pre-conciliar Latin Mass. The Moto Proprio didn't actually make the old Mass legal but made official what already was the case, thereby declaring that it always was the right of priests to say the old Mass without permission from their bishops. After all, if priests today do not need permission to say a Mass that was never mandated, then they certainly don't need permission to say the Mass that was.

If Pope Paul VI had truly mandated the New Mass he would have specified this, but this was never done. Pius V, on the contrary, laid down the law with his subjects in his July, 1570, Constitution on the Mass, saying, "We order them in virtue of holy obedience to chant or to read the Mass according to the rite and manner and norm herewith laid down by Us." He said: "Let Masses not be sung or read according to any other formula than that of this Missal published by Us" mandating that "This new rite alone is to be used."

In the 1969 Missale Romanum, which is the Apostolic Constitution for the promulgation of the Novus Ordo, there is no such mandate for the New Mass or that it even has to be used. The document merely mandates the publication of the new missal with its revised text, ordering that "the prescriptions of this Constitution go into effect November 30th of this year" and that it "be firm and effective now and in the future." But there is no mention of its use.

The decree then validates and makes available the new missal for those who want it. A traditionalist priest of the

SSPX, Father Francois Laisney, points out that "Pope Paul VI did not oblige the use of his [New] Mass, but only permitted it. . . There is no clear order, command, or precept imposing it on any priest!" According to Fr. Laisney, the same applies to subsequent decrees on the New Mass, including the 1971 Notification from the Congregation of Divine Worship, of which he says: "One cannot find in this text any clear prohibition for any other priest to use the traditional Mass nor an obligation to celebrate only the New Mass."

Father Laisney speaks a pure sentence here. In order for a mandate to exist it must be stated what the mandate is. If a centuries old practice is going to be changed and imposed upon the Universal Church that will radically alter the worship of millions, then this needs to be spelled out in clear and juridical terms. Without this done there is no mandate.

The fact that a practice is universally adopted by all the Catholic bishops does not make it a mandate, nor does it necessarily constitute the ordinary practice or teaching of the Church. The Arian Heresy of the fourth century also had the unanimous backing of all the Catholic bishops, and it in fact was mandated upon the people, but there was nothing ordinary about it. "Wrong is wrong even if everyone is doing it", says St. Augustine. The Church's ordinary precepts, as with dogma, are something that God Himself has to bless and guide through His Vicar on earth. This blessing was never given for the New Mass.

The fact is that Paul VI was against the changes in the Mass, but there was little he could do about it. By constantly being pressured by innovators who were trying to exact reforms and signatures out of him, he eventually started to weaken and would even force himself to adopt their arguments of reform in order to console himself, seeing that the coming change was inevitable. But in his heart he knew the changes were immoral and that they would rob the Church of the very thing that had availed it of its active participation with God through the centuries, that being holiness and prayer. Consider his lamentation over the coming promulgation of the New Mass which he delivered at the General Audience of November 26, 1969:

"Newness is going to be noticed, the newness of language. No longer Latin, but the spoken language will be the principal language of the Mass. The introduction of the vernacular will certainly be a *great sacrifice* for those who know the beauty, the power, and the expressive sacrality of Latin. We are parting with the speech of the Christian centuries; we are becoming like profane intruders in the literary preserve of sacred utterance. We will lose a great part of that stupendous and incomparable artistic and spiritual thing, the Gregorian chant. We have reason for regret, reason almost for bewilderment. What can we put in the place of that language of the Angels? We are giving up something of priceless worth. But why? What is more precious than these loftiest of our Church's values?"

Needless to say, the changes in the Mass were not from Pope Paul VI, but were generated by infiltrated Freemasons working through fallen members of the hierarchy. They in turn were the ones who [6]implemented the changes after the Council. Their plan was to heap all the blame on the pope in order to discredit the papacy and drive the good Catholics from the Church so that they could get on with their *Mass destruction* without further censure. It was carefully calculated in their plan to make us think that Paul VI was the modernist culprit who masterminded the New Mass and that the Holy Sacrifice was no longer valid so that loyal Catholics would no longer feel a reason to remain in their parish churches and fight for God's glory.

Pope Paul VI truly was a man of sorrows, seeing that many of his trusted ones were using the Second Vatican Council to misrepresent the Church before the world. There was a plan

---

6   *Through the Congregation of Rites (and others) that Bugnini and the Rhine fathers collaborated with in getting their plan launched. The Bugnini alliance was the moving force behind the implementation of the New Mass.*

afoot at the Council to strip the Mother of God of Her titles and to deny Her role as Mediatrix of all Graces, but the pope stood up in the midst and defended Her dignity and used the Vatican Council to proclaim Her as *Mother of the Church.* There was a move to cast aside the dogma of Papal Infallibility, to dump the *Syllabus of Errors* by Pius IX, and to forsake the Church's 2000 year claim to be the One True Church established by Christ, all of which was a vexation to him.

There was also talk circulating at the Council in favor of birth control which grieved the pope and prompted his valiant rebuttal which came to a triumphant fulfillment on July 25, 1968, when he issued *Humanae Vitae* forbidding any form of artificial contraception. This extraordinary encyclical is historic for the universal impact it has had in saving lives and souls, being the inspired work of God, and has been the very foundation of the Catholic prolife movement of these last times. How is it that there are conservative Catholics who will not recognize the enormous good he did for the advance of traditional family values?

It is true that the pope sought dialogue with other peoples and religions including atheists and Communists, but this outreach proceeded from the purest charity to extend the riches of God to all peoples regardless of race, color or creed. He earnestly desired the friendship of God to rest upon every human on this earth and was never seeking to apologize for the Faith or to adopt their errors into the Church as did the liberal bishops of the Council.

Misrepresented

It was this Vatican confederacy that gave Pope Paul VI a bad name by constantly issuing statements and documents in his name which he had virtually nothing to do with. It is no secret that Cardinal Jean Villot, the Vatican Secretariat from 1969-1979, had often forged his signature and sent out letters purporting to be from Pope Paul, or even had directives issued as coming from the pope which were not from Paul VI.

For instance the pope on September 14, 1972, came down hard on the suggestion made that women might play a role in the priestly ministry with the distribution of sacraments. But on March 29, 1973, the Associated Press reported that "Pope Paul today ruled that women, regardless of whether they are nuns, may distribute Communion in Roman Catholic Churches." Or in May of 1969 the pope through his pastoral letter, *Memoriale Domini,* denounced the practice of receiving Communion in the hand, stating that "the method on the tongue must be retained," yet it wasn't long after this that "Pope Paul" had sanctioned Communion in the hand. With the Vatican's media connection being arranged through the Secretariat office we saw many of Villot's designs being announced in Pope Paul's name.

It's worth recounting the story surrounding the valiant shepherd, Cardinal Mindszenty of Hungary, who suffered imprisonment and torture in his home country for speaking out and defending his flock from the ravages of Communism that were intensifying after WW II. In 1956, as Communism tightened its grip on the Church in Hungary, Cardinal Mindszenty was given asylum at the American Embassy in Budapest where he languished for fifteen years, unable to leave the building, since the agents of Communism awaited him day and night to assassinate him should he leave the embassy.

But on September 28, 1971 the world heard that Cardinal Mindszenty had arrived in Rome at the invitation of Pope Paul VI. He was received with great joy and tenderness by the pope who embraced Cardinal Mindszenty and hung his own pectoral cross around his neck. They both concelebrated Mass and the Holy Father spoke of the Cardinal as **"a guest we have awaited with longing... a symbol of unshakeable strength rooted in faith and in selfless devotion to the Church."**

Again on October 23, 1971, Pope Paul VI concelebrated Mass with Cardinal Mindszenty. The pope gave Mindszenty his own cardinal's mantle and told him in Latin, **"You are and remain Archbishop of Esztergom and Primate of Hungary. Continue working and if you have difficulties, turn trustfully to us!"**

Mindszenty Betrayed

The Cardinal returned to his pastoral cares out in the world, but on February 5, 1974, he received a shocking letter from "Pope Paul" declaring his reign as Archbishop terminated and the See of Esztergom vacant! The Vatican then announced to the world that Cardinal Mindszenty had "retired" to conceal the fact that they had "deposed" him as Mindszenty himself would later testify. His Memoirs end with these words: "This is how I arrived at complete and total exile." The pope of course had nothing to do with his exile.

Given the state of affairs in Rome, the story of Cardinal Mindszenty's removal should come as no surprise. The mutual friendship between Pope Paul and Mindszenty angered the Secretariat since the Office of the Secretariat since 1972 had been committed to [7]protecting the 1962 Moscow-Vatican Treaty which guarantees Vatican respect for Communism, so the dismissal of Mindszenty as the Catholic Primate of Hungary came as a punishment for his open and courageous stand against Communism. The same persecution he received from the Communist officials of Hungary in the 40s and 50s was now being executed through the channels of the Vatican hierarchy.

However, what Mindszenty suffered was relatively minor compared to what Pope Paul had to endure at the hands of

---

7   *Which has also contributed to the silencing of the Fatima Third Secret since the Secret spoke of the enemies of religion that would infiltrate the Church in the latter part of the 20th century.*

these Vatican bureaucrats. The pope was being undermined on every side by those he trusted, with much of this betrayal coming from Bugnini and the liturgists. The following from Kenneth Wolfe's November 2009 article in the New York Times shows to what extent Bugnini was overrunning the papal office:

"Bugnini changed so many things that [Pope] John's successor, Paul VI, sometimes did not know the latest directives. The pope once questioned the vestments set out for him by his staff, saying they were the wrong color, only to be told he [Bugnini] had eliminated the week-long celebration of Pentecost and could not wear the corresponding red garment for Mass. The pope's master of ceremonies then witnessed Paul VI break down in tears."

It was the pope's meekness and dove-like simplicity that irritated the Vatican bureaucracy. In their estimation Pope Paul VI was a fuddy-duddy with no charisma who was preventing the floodgates of the Council from breaking forth. Things were not progressing as smoothly as they wanted because of his immunity to their progressive reform which in 1972 he had identified as the work of the devil. The devil indeed was using these neo-Pharisees as pawns to advance the internal destruction of the Church with Pope Paul VI being the prime object of their attack.

According to the saintly Padre Pio who had paid high tribute to Pope Paul, the Holy Father was being crucified by his own. According to Fr. Malachi Martin who was a brilliant Vatican insider and author of several books, sodomy and satanic sacrifice were being practiced secretly in the Vatican since the time of the Council. According to German author, Theodore Kolberg, there was a double of Pope Paul VI reigning in the Vatican from the mid-seventies on.

These are standard news photos of the two men as they were seen and known in the press as Pope Paul VI. Note the visible difference in the nose. Pope Paul VI (left) has a longer, straighter, more pointed nose, while the impostor (right) has a shorter and rounder nose.

The photos were taken only four years apart, Pope Paul in 1973 (left) and the impostor in 1977 (right). Trick photography was not used in either photograph. The Photos speak for themselves and bear witness to the truth. The four years that lapsed between the two photos would not account for such a drastic difference in appearance.

The existence of an impostor pope in the Vatican during the seventies was common knowledge among diplomatic circles in Rome and is well documented in Kolberg's book, entitled *Der Betrug des Jahrhunderts*. Therein he substantiates his claim with voice-prints and numerous photos of the two popes which show there was a double of Paul VI reigning in the papal village from 1975 on. From what we gather he was an Italian actor of great talent known as *Parr* serving as a puppet under the control of those who had seized control of the Curia in 1972, namely, Cardinals Villot and Benelli, and Cardinal Casaroli (known also for his notorious KGB connections). As we understand it, they drugged the true pope and created this impostor, using the best of plastic surgeons, so that the true pope made very few appearances from that point on.

Left—Pope Paul VI: Long straight nose, almost to the end of ear lobe. Ear is full and round.

Right—the impostor: Nose is shorter and rounder, reaching only 3/4 length of ear. Ear is longer and not as wide.

The reign of an impostor pope would explain the many discrepancies that had confused the faithful concerning Pope Paul VI, for instance why he would condemn the Charismatic Movement in 1969, and why he would embrace it in 1975; or why he would denounce Communion in the hand in May of 1969, and why then he would sanction it from 1975 on. Having an impostor in Rome made it easier for modernists to get on with *their* reform which up to that point had been hampered by the Holy Father's resistance.

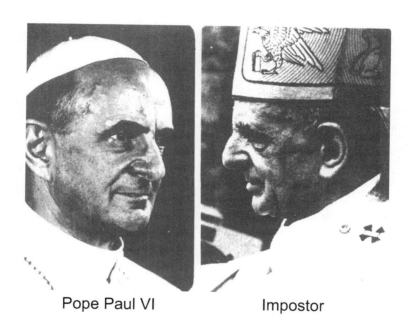

Pope Paul VI   Impostor

If Pope Paul had been in praise of the reform this would have never happened, but as it stands he on occasion would bewail the Council and point out its deplorable fruits. Consider his statement from 1970: "In many areas the Council has not so far given us peace but rather stirred up troubles and problems that in no way serve to strengthen the Kingdom of God within the Church or within its souls." (from Open Letter to Confused Catholics, 1986) Is it any wonder why they crucified him?

Voice Prints—Same Exact Words, Different Voice Signatures

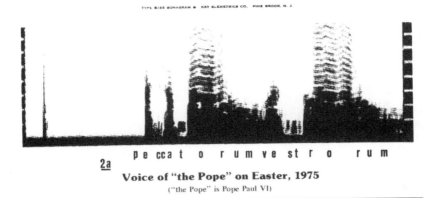

TYPE B/65 SONAGRAM ● KAY ELEMETRICS CO. PINE BROOK, N. J.

pe cca t   o   r u m ve st r   o   r u m

2a

Voice of "the Pope" on Easter, 1975

("the Pope" is Pope Paul VI)

TYPE B/65 SONAGRAM ● KAY ELEMETRICS CO. PINE BROOK, N. J.

pe cca t   o   r u m v e st r   o   r u m

2b

Voice of "the Pope" on Christmas, 1975

("the Pope" is the Imposter)

In his *Umsturz im Vatikan? (An Overthrow in the Vatican?)*, Kolberg presents further evidence for the existence of an impostor pope. Voice recordings of the Latin "Urbi et Urbi" speech of "the Pope" were made on two different occasions. The two recordings were passed through a voice-frequency analyzer made by Kay Elemetrics of Pine Brook, New Jersey. The output Type B/65 sonagram voice-prints of the same words pronounced by the "the Pope" on two different occasions reveal that they were made by two different men. Voice-prints, like finger prints or medical records, are valid evidence that hold up in a court of law.

CONSIDER NOW THE FOLLOWING revelations from the Switzerland exorcisms discussed in the previous chapter wherein the fallen spirits under constraint were forced to speak the truth. The following session is from April 25, 1977 and concerns Pope Paul VI.

E = Exorcist
B = Beelzebub

E: In the name of Jesus, tell the truth, Beelzebub, in the name of the Precious Blood of Jesus Christ, speak!

B: She (the Blessed Virgin) makes me say: Alas! Alas! Some of the cardinals who surround the pope are wolves and...

E: Continue, in the name of Jesus, speak, Beelzebub!

B: We are doing everything to prevent people from becoming aware that there is a second Pope functioning. We are shrewder than all men put together. We are doing everything to keep that hidden... even "traditionalist" priests and lay people do not want to believe it nor to acknowledge it...

E: In the name of Jesus, speak only the truth!

B: For there reigns (in a loud voice) in actual fact, there reigns a false Pope, an imitation Pope... It is important that people are woken up gradually, for they are nearly all asleep.

Pope Paul VI (left) has a longer, more pointed nose compared to the Impostor (right) whose nose is shorter and rounder.

(June 10, 1977)

E: Does Pope Paul VI know that he has a double?

B: At all events, he knows what is going on. He knows... He is suffering unspeakably because, owing to what those cardinals are doing [forging false statements in his name], it is not what Heaven and what he himself would wish which is published in the world and in the Church, and which reaches the bishops. He is very well aware that he is like a prisoner, that he is, as it were, a prisoner of the Vatican. He suffers a great torment because of this.

E: Is the Pope informed about the cardinals? Has he investigated them? In the name of the Most Blessed Virgin Mother of God, tell us the truth!

B: ... He knows everything, everything, but he can do nothing. As we have said, his hands and feet are tied. He can do nothing, he receives injections. The doctor—listen carefully—who treats the Pope, is manipulated in such a way that the Pope receives certain poisons which are harmful to his head and to his mind. But in spite of that, he knows perfectly well what is good… His strength is always so paralyzed, so reduced, that he no longer has the power to stand alone against the others. That is his martyrdom. It is a heavy trial and is permitted from On High. He is, as we have said, a martyr Pope. He who does not believe this will see, his eyes will be opened.

E: How does one recognize the double?

B: We have already had to tell you that previously. Pick up the manuscripts, there is more about it in them than we wanted to say; single out the revelations in which we spoke about the double on earlier occasions, and then read Kolberg's book: "Conspiracy in the Vatican?"

E: Is what Kolberg wrote correct?

B: It is correct.

E: Has Kolberg written the truth? In his book, "Conspiracy in the Vatican?", is he telling the truth?

B: Kolberg tells the truth in his book. He has only a few small things that are not completely correct; but that is not very important.

Bugnini

Let us focus now on the central figure of the liturgical reform, Annibale Bugnini, who from the beginning was the principal draftsman of the New Mass. Naturally the alteration of religion in our time has come about through "principalities and powers" and "the spirits of wickedness in the high places", but Bugnini's position as a liturgist made him a prime tool in the hands of these infernal spirits to start chipping away at the Church's sacrosanct structure.

Bugnini's work as a liturgist goes back to 1947 when he began a twenty-year period as the director of *Ephemerides liturgicae,* one of Italy's best-known liturgical publications. He contributed to numerous scholarly publications, wrote articles on the liturgy for various encyclopedias and dictionaries and had a number of books published on the subject. But there was a hidden agenda at work from the beginning that slowly began to reveal his perditious tracks.

Bugnini had long been in contact with radical members of a liturgical movement which had deviated from the sound principles set forth by Pius X. He was present at a gathering of radical liturgists at Thieulin near Chastres in the late forties of whom Father Duploye, one of those present, writes:

"The Father [Bugnini] listened very attentively, without saying a word, for four days. During our return journey to Paris, as the train was passing along the Swiss Lake at Versailles, he said to me: "I admire what you are doing, but the greatest service I can render you is never to say a word in Rome about all that I have just heard." *(Michael Davies, Liturgical Time Bombs)*

Every indication is that Bugnini was Masonic as we will point out shortly, but Pope John XXIII obviously wasn't aware of this in 1960 when the Preparatory Commission on the Liturgy for the Second Vatican Council was formed, which Bugnini would soon direct. Cardinal Heenan of Westminster even says in his autobiography that "Pope John did not suspect what was being planned by the liturgical experts." If only the pope knew what these liturgical experts were up to!

In 1960 Father Bugnini tragically was placed in a position that enabled him to exert profound influence on the history of the Church when he was appointed Secretary of the Preparatory Commission on the Liturgy. With his position and long standing reputation as a liturgist he was then able to recruit key members of the Rhine coalition to the Commission, whereupon they together drafted what has come to be known as the "Bugnini Schema" on the Mass.

Before the liturgical schema could be presented at the Second Vatican Council for debate, it first had to be approved and signed by Cardinal Gaetano Cicognani, the president of the Preparatory Commission. But when it was submitted to him for approval on January 13, 1962, he immediately detected that the schema contained grave doctrinal dangers that could grow into something disastrous and was having grave misgivings about signing it. So Bugnini immediately arranged (through an appeal to the pope) for pressure to be placed on Cicognani by having the Vatican Secretariat come to the Commission and speak to him with words of persuasion.

One can only imagine the great diabolical pressures being placed on him at that time. The entire assembly of hell must have been present exerting their fullest powers against him, since his signature would put the schema through and open the way for the destruction of the Catholic Church. With the old cardinal practically in tears he finally waved the document in the air and said out loud: "They want me to sign this but I don't know if I want to!" Then he laid the document on his desk, picked up a pen, and signed it. Four days later he died. *(Fr. Ralph Wiltgen, The Rhine Flows Into The Tiber)*

Now that the Bugnini Schema was saved the next step was to present it for discussion at the Second Vatican Council which would take place on October 16, 1962. Of the 72 plus schemata up for discussion the Bugnini Schema was the corrupted one of the set, being embedded with anti-church subtleties, while the others were orthodox and worthy of use. Yet the Bugnini Schema was the one that received rave reviews from the Council while all the others were dumped and never considered! As mentioned before not a trace of the other schemata remained at the Council by the end of the second week. We quote again Archbishop Lefebvre on the matter, this time from another take:

"Now you know what happened at the Council. A fortnight after its opening not one of the prepared schemata remained, not one! All had been turned down, all had been condemned to the wastepaper basket. Nothing remained, not a single sentence. All had been thrown out." *(A Bishop Speaks, Abp Lefebvre, p.131)*

And the rest is history. The Bugnini Schema on the Mass would now be the focus of the Council and became the Constitution on the Sacred Liturgy on December 7, 1962. This in turn became the foundation of the Liturgical Reform that would grow into the Concilium and the other commissions set up to implement the New Mass.

What is interesting to note is that Bugnini was dismissed from two important posts just days after his schema on the Mass was approved. Through the intervention of Cardinal Larraona, Pope John XXIII got wise to his destructive intentions (and sinister connections) and had him removed from his chair at the Lateran University where he taught liturgy and also from his secretaryship to the Liturgical Commission that was to oversee the schema during the conciliar debates. *(Michael*

Davies, *How the Liturgy Fell Apart: The Enigma of Archbishop Bugnini*)

As alluded to earlier, Bugnini's subversive designs were evident long before the Council, for which reason he sometimes was suspected of conspiracy. As far back as 1944 he had asked a Monsignor Arrigo Pintonello to translate some texts on the renewal of liturgy that had been written in part by German Protestants. His protestant connection is highlighted in a sermon delivered by His Excellency Bishop Lazo of the Philippines on Ascension Thursday, 1998:

"I discovered the real reason for the illegal suppression of the Traditional Latin Mass. The ancient Mass was an obstacle to the introduction of Ecumenism. The Catholic Mass contained Catholic dogmas, which Protestants denied. To achieve unity with protestant sects, the Tridentine Latin Mass had to be scrapped, being replaced by the Novus Ordo Missae. The Novus Ordo Missae was a concoction of Monsignor Annibale Bugnini, a Freemason. Six protestant ministers helped Monsignor Bugnini in fabricating it. The innovators saw to it that no Catholic dogmas offensive to protestant ears were left in the prayers. They deleted all that expressed the Catholic dogmas fully and replaced them with very ambiguous, protestantizing, and heretical things."

In the March 19, 1965 issue of *L' Osservatore Romano,* Archbishop Bugnini said, "We must strip from our Catholic prayers and from the Catholic liturgy everything which can be the shadow of a stumbling-block for our separated brethren. . . the Protestants."

We can understand why Archbishop Lefebvre declared the following in his *Letter to Friends and Benefactors* in March of 1976: "Now, when we hear in Rome that he who was the heart and soul of the liturgical reform is a Freemason, we may think that he is not the only one. The veil covering the greatest deceit ever to have mystified the clergy and baffled the faithful is doubtless beginning to be torn asunder."

As a little example of Bugnini's deceptive workings in the Vatican, we cite you this little anecdote from 1974. The Consilium for the Reform of the Liturgy had in its ranks a number of liturgists including a Father Louis Bouyer who was opposed to the changes in the Mass. Bugnini argued his cause with Father Bouyer by telling him that Pope Paul VI wanted the new changes in the Mass, and then Bugnini told Pope Paul that Bouyer and the 'Consilium experts' had decided in favor of these changes. Obviously it was Bugnini who wanted the changes and Pope Paul later acknowledged to Fr. Bouyer that Bugnini had deceived both of them. The following is an interview that took place between Pope Paul VI and Fr. Bouyer in 1974.

(Father Louis Bouyer)—I wrote to the Holy Father, Pope Paul VI, to tender my resignation as member of the Commission charged with the Liturgical Reform. The Holy Father sent for me at once and the following conversation ensued:

Paul VI: Father, you are an unquestionable and unquestioned authority by your deep knowledge of the Church's liturgy and Tradition, and a specialist in this field. I do not understand why you have sent me your resignation, whilst your presence, is more than precious, it is indispensable!

Father Bouyer: Most Holy Father, if I am a specialist in this field, I tell you very simply that I resign because I do not agree with the reforms you are imposing! Why do you take no notice of the remarks we send you, and why do you do the opposite?

Paul VI: But I don't understand: I'm not imposing anything. I have never imposed anything in this field. I have complete trust in your competence and your propositions. It is you who are sending me proposals. When Fr. Bugnini comes to see me, he says: "Here is what the experts are asking for." And as you are an expert in this matter, I accept your judgment.

Father Bouyer: When we have studied a question, and have chosen what we can propose to you, in conscience, Father Bugnini took our text, and, then said to us that, having consulted you: "The Holy Father wants you to introduce these changes into the liturgy." And since I don't agree with your propositions, because they break with the Tradition of the Church, then I tender my resignation.

Paul VI: But not at all, Father, believe me, Father Bugnini tells me exactly the contrary: I have never refused a single one of your proposals. Father Bugnini came to find me and said: "The experts of the Commission charged with the Liturgical Reform asked for this and that." And since I am not a liturgical specialist, I tell you again, I have always accepted your judgment. I never said that to Monsignor Bugnini. I was deceived. Father Bugnini deceived me and deceived you.

Father Bouyer: That is, my dear friends, how the liturgical reform was done!

(*The original French version of this early 1970s conversation between Father Bouyer and Pope Paul VI was translated by Father Anthony Chadwick who found the original version at this website: http://www.leforumcatholique.org/message. php?num=508624:*)

It's significant to note that Pope Paul reposed complete confidence in Father Bouyer's judgment on liturgical matters and was happy to let him exert his influence on the Consilium for the retention of Tradition in the Mass. Unfortunately, Fr. Bouyer yielded to pressure from other liturgists and eventually dropped out of the Consilium.

Masonic Connection

It suffices to say that Pope Paul was not the wolf, but was a lamb among the brethren, though he unfortunately was a bit naive. One of his virtuous faults was his unwillingness to see the evil in his fellow man, which unfortunately permitted certain evil ones to carry on in Rome. The Holy Father on occasion had been briefed about Bugnini's affiliation with the Freemasons but he would hear none of it.

But in July of 1975 the pope was forced against his will to learn of Bugnini's affiliation with the Freemasons. Bugnini had attended a meeting with the Secretariat of State where he forgot his briefcase. A dossier obtained from Bugnini's briefcase was personally brought to Pope Paul VI by a reputable high cardinal who had obtained it from a monsignor who had opened the briefcase to see who it belonged to. The dossier contained private instructions from the Masonic Grand Master in Italy to Bugnini which convinced Pope Paul beyond any shadow of a doubt that he was a Freemason. The following is part of what Pope Paul read from the dossier and is dated June 14, 1964:

"Dear Buan [Masonic code name of Bugnini]:

"We communicate the task appointed to you by the Council of Brothers, in accordance with the Grand Master and the Assistant Princes to the Throne. We oblige you to spread de-Christianization by confusing rites and languages and to set priests, bishops and cardinals against each other.

Linguistic and ritualistic babel means victory for us, since linguistic and ritual unity has been the strength of the Church... Everything must happen within a decade."

Note the satanic strategy for defeating Christians: To divide is to conquer! The following now is a [8]letter from Bugnini to the Grand Master of the lodge updating him on the progress of his secret mission. This is dated July 2, 1967.

"Incomparable Grand Master: The de-sacralization is rapidly taking place. Another Instruction was published, which took effect on June 29. We can already sing victory, because the vulgar language is sovereign in the whole liturgy, including the essential parts. . . The greatest liberty was given to choose between the various formulas, to individual creativity, and to chaos! In short, with this document I believe to have spread the principle of maximum licentiousness, in accordance with your wishes.

"I fought hard against my enemies from the Congregation for the Rites, and I had to use all my astuteness so that the Pope would approve it. By luck, we found the support of friends and brothers in Universa Laus *[International Association for the Study of Liturgical Music]*, who are faithful. I thank you for the funds sent and am waiting to see you soon. I embrace you,

Your Brother Buan."

---

8   *This correspondence is taken from Andrea Tornielli's "Dossie Liturgia Uma Babel Programada," that appeared in the June 1992 issue of 30 Days. It coincides with Tito Casini's blockbuster book of April 1976, "In the Smoke of Satan-Towards the Final Clash," in which the author states: "The reform has been conducted by this Bugnini who has been unmasked at last; he is indeed what we long expected: a Freemason." Casini here was reporting on the 'dossier' incident of July 1975 that caused Bugnini to be expelled from the Vatican that summer (see p. 53).*

An Example of Mass Confusion Envisioned by Bugnini

Traditionalist Catholic writer, Michael Davies, investigated the allegations against Bugnini and made contact with the priest who had discovered the dossier in Bugnini's briefcase and who had "this information placed in the hands of Pope Paul VI by a cardinal." The matter is discussed at some length in his book, *How the Liturgy Fell Apart: The Enigma of Archbishop Bugnini,* wherein he shows how the pope at this point was convinced of Bugnini's affiliation with the Masonic lodge.

The story about the briefcase also appeared in Piers Compton's 1981 book *The Broken Cross.* Therein he states that Bugnini's Masonic membership was recorded in "The Italian Register" on April 23, 1963, "and that his code name was Buan."

As a result of Pope Paul's shocking discovery, Bugnini was suddenly dismissed as the head of the Congregation of Divine Worship, whereupon the Congregation itself was dissolved and merged with a new Congregation for the Sacraments which Bugnini wasn't even permitted to join. This occurred in July, 1975. Thereupon a plan was in motion to send him into a sort of exile by making him 'papal nuncio' of Iran which was announced in the press shortly thereafter.

Archbishop Annibale Bugnini

The Freemasons of course are a satanic secret society committed solely to destroying the Catholic Church. Their practice of witchcraft, murder and devil worship is no secret, for which reason the Church has always forbidden any association with them. Those who join them are accursed.

If anyone would doubt the diabolical nature of the Freemasons, let him consider the testimony of Albert Pike (1809-1891), the American high priest of Freemasonry who was elected in 1859 as Sovereign Grand Commander of the Southern Supreme Council, Ancient and Accepted Scottish Rite, and who later became Provincial Grand Master of the Grand Lodge of the Royal Order of Scotland in the United States. He addressed fellow initiates with the following:

"To the crowd we must say: we worship a God, but it is the God one adores without superstition. To you, Sovereign Grand Inspectors, we say this, that you may repeat it to the brethren of the 32nd, 31st and 30th degrees: all of us initiates of the high degrees should maintain the Masonic religion in the purity of the Luciferian doctrine. If Lucifer were not God, would Adonay, the God of the Christians [Jesus Christ], whose deeds prove his cruelty, perfidy and hatred of man, his barbarism and repulsion for science, would Adonay and his priests calumniate him? Yes, Lucifer is God, and unfortunately Adonay is also God. Religious philosophy in its purity and truth consists in the belief in Lucifer, the equal of Adonay." (Albert Pike, as quoted in A. C. de la Rive: La Femme et l'Enfant dans la Franc-Maconnerie Universelle, page 588.)

There have actually been a number of Freemasons in the Vatican since the Council, but we only mention Bugnini above because of his central role in changing the Mass and because the evidence on him is more readily available. In 1974 he even proclaimed the liturgical reform of the Second Vatican Council to be "a major conquest of the Catholic Church."

To think that the powers of darkness could exert so much power in the upper echelons of the Eternal City! It was this very situation that eventually compelled Pope Paul VI to make his mega-statement of October 13, 1977: "The tail of the devil is functioning in the disintegration of the Catholic world. The darkness of Satan has entered and spread throughout the Catholic Church even to its summit. Apostasy, the loss of the Faith, is spreading throughout the world and into the highest levels within the Church." (The 60th Anniversary of Our Lady's last appearance at Fatima)

The apostasy lamented here was the fruit of the Council design to open its doors and unite the Church with the world. The pirates starting blowing holes in the ship whereby the polluted sea of the world started to seep in. A false ecumenism prevailed that allowed outsiders and representatives of other religions to sit in on the Council and help direct the building of a new church.

The end result has been a pacifist surrender to the world. The Church in our time has yielded to the currents of change and secular thought, fulfilling St. John's prophecy that the Holy City would be overrun by the Gentiles for a symbolic time of forty two months. (Apocalypse 11:2) The temple today is now a place of traffic for the advance of secular enterprise that has served to destroy the awareness of the supernatural presence of Christ in His sanctuary. The reform didn't pan out as expected, but only produced the fools gold of novelty which in turn nurtured contempt for the true gold of Tradition. "By their fruits you shall know them." (Matthew 7:20)

Liturgy as a Tool

As an example of how the liturgy can be used to enlighten or deceive souls it is worth examining briefly the Consecration, since this is the high point of the Mass around which the entire liturgy revolves. During the Consecration the Sacrifice of Jesus Christ is reenacted on the altar through the commemorative formula commanded by Christ to His Apostles—**This is My Body, This is My Blood**—so that His Body, Blood, Soul and Divinity become truly and entirely present. The Mass is not a symbol or mere commemoration of Calvary but is the actual event of Calvary that took place 2000 years ago, though it be mystical and unbloody.

Upon elevation of the bread and chalice the substance of bread and wine is changed into the very substance of Jesus

Christ so that the substance of the bread and wine ceases to exist. It is now the substance of Jesus Christ, only and entirely, without any other substance mingling with it. Only the accidents or physical properties of bread and wine remain (e.g. taste, smell, touch) but the substance itself is now Christ, and only Christ. This Divine substance under the appearance of bread and wine is what we call **The Mystery of Faith.**

The very purpose of the liturgy is to propose this Divine Eucharistic Mystery for our belief where the wording imparts light and reverence concerning this Mystery so that we are aware of the supernatural presence of Christ on the altar. The acknowledgement of this supernatural Mystery is the first and foremost requirement placed on us by the Church in order to receive Holy Communion, without which one may not receive Communion. Every word of Holy Mass is like a censor rendering honor and glory to this Most Holy Sacrament of the altar, especially the words in and around the Consecration.

Immediately following the Consecration wherein occurs this Mystery the Old Rite of the Mass resumes most appropriately with these words, "And Now, O Lord, we, Thy servants, and with us all Thy holy people, calling to mind the blessed Passion of this same Christ, Thy Son, our Lord, likewise His Resurrection from the grave, and also his glorious Ascension into heaven, do offer unto Thy most sovereign Majesty out of the gifts Thou hast bestowed upon us, a Victim..."

Whereas the New Mass following Consecration attempts to proclaim the Mystery of Faith, which it does erroneously. The following text follows in the original 1969 version of the New Rite:

"Let us proclaim the Mystery of Faith: Christ has died, Christ is risen, Christ will come again"

What is proclaimed here is not The Mystery of Faith and has nothing to do with it and to proclaim it as such with conviction would be heresy. Yet, for the past forty years this is what has been proclaimed as the 'Mystery of Faith.' Modernist reformers deliberately inserted these words at the end of Consecration to destroy our conception of this Divine Mystery and place it completely out of mind.

Generally the new liturgy seeks to divert us away from this awesome and mysterious reenactment of Christ's Sacrifice, the best example of this being the 'sign of peace' just before Communion which was proposed under the guise of *Restoration of Liturgy.* Here Christ has just been called upon the altar (through the priest) where He is present in His Sacrifice, pleading our cause in sorrow. It is a most sacred moment leading into that intimate time of the Mass when we will receive Him in person.

And of course, the purpose of the liturgy is to call us into active participation in the Holy Sacrifice, that we might be absorbed with His Passion and be one with Him so that we can be purified of our defects and have our sins forgiven. During this time there should not be a thought or ambitious notion that crosses the mind, but only silence and compunction mingled with joyful anticipation of what we are about to receive.

But then cometh the Modernists with their rude infringement: 'Hey Jack, peace be with you buddy, how's your girl friend, hey we'll see you guys after Mass, etc., etc.' And of course the socialist festivity will often continue up to the Communion rails and beyond with a little help from the guitar ensemble to spur them on, to the end that the people are scandalized. The acknowledgment of The True Presence is destroyed.

The sign of peace was deliberately inserted just before Communion to destroy our Communion and divert us away from Christ. It in fact is a protestant practice and is among those prized reformist "elements which have suffered injury through accidents of history" which have now been "restored." It coincides with the new Vatican II definition of the Mass being

"A service and a collegial, ecumenical communion."

Bugnini and his team deliberately created little weak spots or openings in the liturgy with the view that they would eventually go off like liturgical time-bombs in the future, a good example of this being the sign of peace just mentioned. What originally started as a simple and courteous hand shake (as is still done in many parishes) has blown up into a full fledged rock concert in some parishes where the music and clapping will go for a full 2 or 3 minutes before they resume with the Communion, if in fact it ever stops.

We have a similar situation with the *responsorial psalms* between readings which was just another modernist invention to get the people jacked up in the *Spirit of the Council.* This new innovation creates a break of continuity in the Mass which opens the door to festive or musical interludes where the congregation sometimes will clap and sing for a full three minutes to the beat of a pop ensemble strumming near the altar, led by a woman in a sleazy, low-cut outfit. This is the new progressive way of leading the people in "prayer."

Another scandal of Council reformers was their perfidious attempt to eliminate Latin from the liturgy. While feigning to honor Latin as the established liturgical language, the conciliar documents actually grant that Latin can be thrown out in place of the vernacular if it will pacify the people and elicit their "active participation." Take for instance article 36 of the Concilium:

"Since the use of the mother tongue [vernacular], whether in the Mass, the administration of the sacraments, or other parts of the liturgy, frequently may be of great advantage to the people, the limits of its employment may be extended." [2]

The resulting switch from Latin to vernacular has been a major contributing factor in the present day disunity in the Church. Because with the Mass said today in the language of each country, this has fostered the idea that the Church is something that is secular and divided, as opposed to holy and universal. So a return of the old Latin Rite is needed to restore unity to the Church as it existed before Vatican II.

But it's also needed to restore a sense of reverence for the Eucharistic Mystery that occurs at every Mass. The new formulas are base and novel and suggest that the Eucharist is earthly food and drink that God blesses. Take for instance: "Blessed are you, Lord God of all creation, for through your goodness we have received the wine we offer you: fruit of the vine and work of human hands, it will become our spiritual drink." (From the New Missal)

The Liturgy then is a powerful element to condition the faithful for better or for worse, and has been the primary means of Modernists to impart a new theology to the faithful. As Monsignor Gamber states in his book: "This is why a new rite was created, a rite that in many ways reflects the bias of the new [modernist] theology. The traditional liturgy simply could not be allowed to exist in its established form because it was permeated with the truths of the traditional faith and the ancient forms of piety. For this reason alone, much was abolished and new rites, prayers and hymns were introduced, as were the new readings from Scripture, which conveniently left out those passages that did not square with the teachings of modern theology." (The Reform of the Roman Liturgy, p. 100)

Revelations

"God has willed that external proofs of His revelation, namely divine acts and especially miracles and prophecies, should be added to the internal aids given by the Holy Spirit. Since these proofs so excellently display God's omnipotence and limitless knowledge, they constitute the surest signs of divine revelation, signs that are suitable to everyone's understanding."

—The First Vatican Council

Marie-Julie Jahenny
(1850-1941)
Mystic of the Holy Catholic Church

In discussing the internal subversion of the Church it behooves us to cite the revelations of those who have had the most penetrating insight into the matter, namely, the mystics. God's concern in this area is being echoed through his servants of the last times in keeping with Amos 3:7: "For the Lord God doth nothing without revealing his secret to his servants, the prophets."

Marie Julie Jahenny is an approved mystic of the Catholic Church who prophesied the modern changes to the Mass over a hundred years ago. Her bishop, Monsignor Fourier of Nantes, not only sanctioned but promoted her revelations, seeing that they had great spiritual value for the Church. Her message is along the same lines as the message of La Salette concerning the great apostasy and profanation of the last times, which according to the seer would bring a great and horrific punishment upon humanity.

Marie Julie Jahenny was given a vision of a dialogue between Christ and Lucifer in which the latter said:

"I will attack the Church. I will overthrow the Cross, I will decimate the people, I will deposit a great weakness of Faith in hearts. There will also be a great denial of religion. For a time I will be master of all things, everything will be under my control, even Your temple and all Your people."

[Marie-Julie] —"There will not remain any vestige of the Holy Sacrifice, no apparent trace of faith. Confusion will be everywhere...All the works approved by the infallible Church will cease to exist as they are today for a time."

On November 27, 1902, Our Lord announced the conspiracy to invent a "New Mass."

"I give you a warning. The disciples who are not of My Gospel are now working hard to remake according to their ideas and under the influence of the enemy of souls a Mass that contains words that are odious in My sight! When the fatal hour arrives when the faith of my priests is put to the test, it will be these texts [new missal] that will be celebrated in this second period. The first period is the one of my priesthood which exists since Me. The second is the one of the persecution when the enemies of the Faith and of Holy Religion will impose their formulas in the book of the second celebration. Many of My holy priests will refuse this book, sealed with the words of the abyss. Unfortunately, amongst them are those who will accept it. These infamous spirits are those who crucified me and are awaiting the kingdom of the new messiah."

ONE OF THE MOST revealing and timely messages of the 20th century was from a humble Mexican nun whom Christ wanted known as his little "Portovaz" messenger. Unlike the above seer, these revelations were neither approved nor disapproved but the message stands on its own merits and speaks for itself. The following revelation is from March 24, 1969, and concerns the New Mass and Pope Paul VI:

"All of you have permitted My enemy to enter My Church. The Bark of Peter flounders on the sea of human life. It may seem as though I am asleep. But it is not so—I am not asleep. On the contrary, I keep constant watch over My Beloved Spouse [the Church] to whom I have promised Eternal Life.

"Before the time of the harvest arrives, I order, I command that you do two things: see to it that the modern Masses shall immediately cease; and, return to the Canon decreed in the Council of Trent by Pius V.

"Return to the primitive fountains of the Church. Restore the Christian and religious customs among seculars and religious, and repent, all of you who belong to the Hierarchy of My Church! All of you who have apostatized and have become traitors, repent and retrace your steps to the right way! And of course, this must be done immediately!

"To come to Me is to confess humbly that My doctrine is holy and that it does not need reforms, that My Church is divine, and that all must come to her bosom if they wish to be saved eternally. It means to confess her royal dignity which shines through Me, from Peter to My present Vicar, my much loved Paul VI. They must obey him! Let them not pressure him, nor exact from him reforms for My Church!

"My Church is holy and I remain permanently in her, even though there should remain in her only one single man who would know how to observe My doctrine purely and completely. My Church has rules of life to which all of you must subject yourselves in humble submission.

"Demagogy, astuteness, error and falsehood are contained in all the so-called sociological techniques proposed by the innovators, who are fighting to supplant My doctrine and My Church. All of these are brimming over with satanic evil, the evil which the spirit of Satan has infiltrated into them…

"The definitions which have been (decreed) from other centuries and which have been approved must not be abrogated nor changed. Let Paul VI speak the truth to the face of the world and let him confess that they have pressured him and obligated him into many present-day definitions which he in his heart has not accepted…

"Paul VI suffers! Do not leave him alone in his prison. Go in search of him! Take him out of there to a safe place where he may be able to speak freely, according to the motion and light of My Spirit. Then you shall see that he is loyal to My doctrine and that his soul overflows with charity emanated from My heart…

"Tell them it is repugnant to me that they receive Holy Communion standing and without reverence. Tell them that I am offended by those who receive Holy Communion cynically, giving bad example, by the women who approach with heads uncovered and naked bodies!"

THE APPROVED REVELATIONS of Our Lady of La Salette (1846) also prophesied the crisis of the last times, stating that "Rome will lose the Faith and become the seat of Antichrist." This prophecy concerning Antichrist referenced the reign of disobedience that would surround the Holy Father and the darkness of spirit that would hang over the Eternal City on account of it.

Contrary to rumors fabricated by infidels, the message of La Salette (short form) was approved by Pope Pius IX in 1851 after being submitted to him by the bishop of La Salette, France, where the apparitions occurred. So much did he endorse the message that he dissuaded the seer, Melanie Calvat, from becoming a nun on the grounds that this would take away from her mission to propagate the La Salette message in the world. Melanie explains in her memoirs: "His Holiness Pius IX relieved me of such vows as could not be kept in the world; he said that I couldn't accomplish my mission in the cloister and he granted me privileges I would never have dared ask him."

Melanie was viciously persecuted by the Masonically controlled clergy of France who resented her revelations, since they had convicted them of their betrayal against the Faith. Badgered beyond endurance, she fled to Italy where she earnestly sought to publish the full Secret of La Salette under the Bishop of Naples, which took place in 1879 with the stamp of imprimatur.

Pope Leo XIII, who wholeheartedly embraced her visions, then called Melanie to Rome to confer with her about private messages she had received concerning a religious order of the future that would be instrumental in restoring the Catholic Church. He was deeply interested in this because he saw what was coming upon the Church and was most zealous to employ any remedies to hold off the coming onslaught of modernism, to which end he kept her in Rome for six months finalizing the details for the constitution of this new religious order. With this same concern, he also [9]composed the famous Prayer to St. Michael with the mandate that it be said after the low Masses, since he knew that the protection of this Heavenly warrior was needed for the Church of the future.

Unfortunately, the good pope never lived to see his desired religious order, but he did everything in his power to act in the spirit of that order, even issuing his outstanding encyclical on Freemasonry on April 20, 1884, *Humanum Genus,* which exposed the satanic plots of the Freemasons against the Catholic Church. The behavior they promote among our Catholic clergy is described in the following excerpt from the La Salette prophecy, which is applicable to our time.

"The priests, ministers of My Son, the priests, by their wicked lives, by their irreverence and their impiety in the celebration of the holy mysteries, by their love of money, their love of honors and pleasures, the priests have become cesspools of impurity. Yes, the priests are asking vengeance, and vengeance is hanging over their heads. Woe to the priests and to those dedicated to God who by their unfaithfulness and their wicked lives are crucifying My Son again! The sins of those dedicated to God cry out towards Heaven and call for vengeance, and now vengeance is at their door, for there is no one left to beg mercy and forgiveness for the people. There are no more generous souls; there is no one left worthy to offer a stainless sacrifice to the Eternal for the sake of the world.

God will strike in an unprecedented way.

"Woe to the inhabitants of the earth! God will exhaust His wrath upon them and no one will be able to escape so many

---

9   *This was actually prompted by a miracle he received on October 13, 1884, wherein he heard the devil tell Christ that he would destroy His Church within a hundred years.*

afflictions together. The chiefs, the leaders of the people of God have neglected prayer and penance, and the devil has bedimmed their intelligence. They have become wandering stars which the old devil will drag along with his tail to make them perish." (Apocalypse 12: 4)

Melanie's integrity as a seer was evidenced by her holiness of life, as described by her last spiritual director, Fr. Rigaux, who tells it as it is: "In the 48 years that I've been a priest, I've known and directed some very beautiful souls. I dare state before God, who will soon judge me, that never have I encountered a soul so humble, gentle, pure, obedient, a virgin so pure, a character so strong, a victim so resigned in frightful trials, a martyr in body, bearing the stigmata from her tenderest years."

It is good to point out that the abrogation of Canon Laws 2318 & 1399 by Pope Paul VI in 1966 gives all Catholics the freedom to propagate unapproved revelations without having to wait for the formal sanction of the Church. The Church now grants the faithful this freedom on the condition that there is nothing in the material that goes against Catholic faith and morals.

ANOTHER REVELATION worth mentioning are the messages of Bayside, New York, transmitted through the late seer, Veronica of the Cross (1970-1995). Because of their conservatism and censure of homosexuality, the revelations did not meet the criteria of the Brooklyn bishop, Francis Mugavero, for which reason he refused to investigate the apparitions. As such, his November 1986 statement on Bayside remains null and void as faithful Catholics from far and wide continue to frequent the apparition site in good faith.

Vatican Pavilion Site in Flushing Meadows Park, New York
Pilgrims gather throughout the year at the holy grounds in witness of the apparition which continues to make its impact upon the international faith community. Noteworthy clergy have gone on record as endorsing Bayside, including the late Father John Hardon who was perhaps the greatest American theologian of the 20th century, as well as the late Father Malachi Martin who was a brilliant author and adviser to three popes who had read the Third Secret of Fatima. (The complete information available at www.smwa.org)

As stated earlier, the Third Secret prophecy referenced the internal destruction of the Church that would unfold in the latter part of the 20th century. Among those who have read and commented on the Secret we find a common thread in that it concerned the great apostasy of the last times and how the infiltration of heresy would begin at the top (Vatican Curia) and filter down to the man in the pew. On May 13, 1978, the Blessed Virgin Herself gave us the gist of the Fatima Third Secret:

"They converse of the secret that I gave at Fatima. It is a simple explanation. It could not be fully revealed because of the drastic nature of My message. How I warned and warned that satan would enter into the highest realms of the hierarchy in Rome. The Third Secret, My child, is that satan would enter into My Son's Church."

We mentioned before, too, how the dark forces had initially besieged and overtaken the Second Vatican Council, and how this plan was kicked into play on day three of the Council when the vote needed to determine the members of the conciliar commissions was suddenly blocked, allowing radical progressives to capture a controlling number of seats on the Council. This historic takeover of Vatican II took place on October 13, 1962, the 45th Anniversary of the Virgin Mary's last apparition at Fatima. Consider the following revelation from Jesus to Veronica, on June 18, 1986:

"On that date, as promised at Fatima, satan entered My Church upon earth. He brought with him his agents—and satan himself, the deceiver of all mankind—sat in on Vatican II, and maneuvered all the outsiders to come in and distort My doctrines and distort the truth."

The message lamented the Blessed Virgin's "great hurt and sorrow that Her message at Fatima was not completely given to mankind" since it concerned the subversion of the hierarchy through which many would be misled. Consider the following:

"With Vatican II, it started out with the best resolves, but then satan took over the scene. And with his agents he reached into the highest professions, the highest league of the hierarchy, until, it saddens Me to say that many priests now are on the road to perdition and taking many others with them." (Jesus, July 25, 1985)

This echoes still an earlier message from July 25, 1977: "The Council of Vatican II was started with good intent, but the doors were opened to all manner of heretics, causing a slow pollution of the Faith."

"I will stake my reputation on the doctrine contained in the messages"

—Father Robert Skurla,
former International Fatima Blue Army chaplain

On September 27, 1975, it was stated, "You must go back in the immediate years and bring the knowledge to mankind that these changes, the changes that have given bad fruits have not been given to you through the Holy Spirit and through your Vicar, Pope Paul VI. It is the web of satan reaching out." This same message went on to reveal:

The Deception of the Century

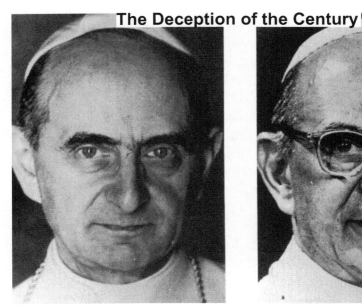

"My child, I bring to you a sad truth, one that must be made known to mankind. In doing this, My child, you must proceed without fear. It must be made known to mankind. Our dear beloved Vicar,

Pope Paul VI, he suffers much at the hands of those he trusts. My child, shout it from the rooftops. He is not able to do his mission. They have laid him low, My child. He is ill, he is very ill. Now there is one who is ruling in his place, an impostor, created from the minds of the agents of satan. Plastic surgery, My child—the best of surgeons were used to create this impostor. Shout from the rooftops! He must be exposed and removed.

"Behind him, My child, there are three who have given themselves to satan. You do not receive the truth in your country and the world. Your Vicar is a prisoner.

Cardinal Casaroli   Cardinal Villot   Cardinal Benelli

"Antonio Casaroli, you shall condemn your soul to hell! Giovanni Benelli, what road have you taken? You are on the road to hell and damnation! [10] Villot, leader of evil, take yourself from among those traitors; you are not unknown to the Eternal Father. You consort with the synagogue of satan. Do you think you shall not pay for the destruction of souls in My Son's House?

---

10 *On August 21, 1974, she also said, "V does much damage to the Holy Father by changing his correspondence. V rewrites his letters. V censors his mail." On September 27, 1975, she said, "You cannot accept now what comes from Rome, for they do not come, these bulls, and these directions are not written by the pen of Pope Paul VI. They are written by the pen of Benelli and Villot."*

"The Antichrist, the forces of evil, have gathered, My children, within the Eternal City. You must make it known to mankind that all that is coming from Rome is coming from darkness. The light has not passed that way. The appearance in public is not Paul VI, it is the impostor pope. Medication of evil has dulled the brain of the true Pope, Pope Paul VI. They send into his veins poison to dull his reasoning and paralyze his legs. What evil creature have you opened the doors to the Eternal City and admitted? The agents of satan! You plan to remove the Eternal Father from your heart and the hearts of those whom you seek to deceive. You scatter the flock.

"My children, you must now pray for the light. You must know the truth. All that is given to you is being sent from the traitorous heart of those who have seized power in the Eternal City of Rome."

NEEDLESS TO SAY, we see the Church today in a state of revolt, which will materialize fully when we see all out revolution in the streets of Rome. According to the message, this outbreak of revolution in the Eternal City will be our cue that a great and magnificent Warning from the heavens is about to occur on earth. "When you see, when you hear, when you feel the revolution in Rome, when you see the Holy Father fleeing, seeking a refuge in another land, know that the time is ripe." (Jesus, September 14, 1976)

The Warning will be a worldwide cataclysmic occurrence of unprecedented magnitude that will shake the entire planet. This event will be seen and experienced everywhere by all peoples and will be universally acknowledged as having come from God. During the Warning every person living will be made to see exactly where he stands with God at that time. "Man will feel that the very powers of the elements have shaken the very foundations of his being, so great will be the impact of this Warning from the Father. But none shall doubt that it had come from the Father." (Our Lady, September 28, 1974)

We are told in the message that the coming intervention is warranted by the widespread decadence and degeneracy of our time, though the profanation of the temple in particular is what is inciting this divine action upon our world. According to the message, this will fall hard on the clergy who use their rank to chip away at the Church's foundation and build toward a new religion. Jesus tells the clergy: "You must now return to your traditional rites! You must restore My House from its crumbling exterior and rotting interior! You must rebuild what you seek to destroy—now!" (Jesus, November 22, 1975)

According to the message, innovators forfeit their salvation. "All who seek reform and change will not receive a sanctification from Heaven. Reform and you will die on the vine!" (May 23, 1979) The just on the other hand will be worry-free. "All who remain in the light of grace will have no fear. They will pass through this great Warning without suffering." (April 5, 1975)

The message also speaks of the establishment of a coming religious order that will be instrumental in restoring the Church. "This order will be founded on basic tradition. This order will gather those of true spirit. This order will be composed of both men and women, and a cloistered convent... It will be a refuge in the time of trial for many. This refuge will be located, My child, in your country, the United States." (Our Lady, November 20, 1974)

Back in the 1970s, Veronica, under Heavenly guidance, established the Lay Order of St. Michael, a celibate group of men dedicated to bringing the Bayside prophecies to the world. We are told in the message that from this lay order will emerge the full fledged religious Order of St. Michael which will lead the cause for the restoration in the last times, assisted by the Discalced Carmelites and the Franciscans. On May 22, 1974, the Holy Virgin said:

"The Order of Michael will be established in the United States"

(Quotations provided by www.smwa.org which is the official website for the Bayside mission. Information available from St Michael's World Apostolate, P.O. Box 514, Bayside NY, 11361)

The True Altar

It suffices to say that we are living in desperate times when the powers of darkness are waging their final battle against the Church. We are witnessing today the profanation of the temple prefigured by the profanation in the time of Antiochus the Illustrious (175-164 BC) when the priests of the temple departed the religion of their fathers and assisted the heathens in setting up their idols in the sanctuary. We read how Judas Machabees and his men went into the temple and threw down their idols and pagan altars and set the true altar of God back up. (Machabees 1-2) This also prefigured how the elect of the last times would assist their leader in restoring the true altar.

The true altar, of course, is the high altar [11] facing east away from the people *(ad orientum)* that was in use from the Third Century on when marble churches were first built. But this was taken away at Vatican II in keeping with Chapter V of [12] *Inter Oecumenici* which outlined the new ruling for the sanctuary:

"The main altar should preferably be freestanding, to permit walking around it and celebration facing the people. Its location in the place of worship should be truly central so that the attention of the whole congregation naturally focuses there." [article 91]

---

11 *According to scholars it was the liturgical practice of St. Peter and the Apostles that laid the groundwork for this manner of constructing altars. The popes since the fifth century have consistently argued that the traditional Roman Canon originated with the Apostle Peter.*

12 *The Vatican instruction, Institutio Generalis Missalis, also established guidelines for Mass facing the people (article 299).*

A key objective in having the altar "freestanding" and "central" was to allow the people to "gather around the table of the Lord" so that it would enhance their "active participation" as "a holy priesthood" in the "breaking of bread." This also achieves the modernist objective of seeing the Mass now as a "community meal."

According to Monsignor Gamber the turning around of the altars was the most destructive reform since the Council, citing that "there is no basis for it in liturgical history, nor theology, nor sociologically." He points out that "changes in the traditional liturgy also mean a change of faith itself" and goes on to say:

"The focus must forever be on God, not man. This has always meant that everyone turn towards Him in prayer, rather than that the priests face the people. From this

insight, we must draw the necessary conclusion and admit that the celebration versus populum is, in fact, an error. In the final analysis, celebration versus populum is a turning towards man, and away from God."

Monsignor Gamber also states: "A real change in the contemporary perception of the purpose of the Mass and the Eucharist will occur only when the table altars are removed and Mass is again celebrated at the high altar; when the purpose of the Mass is again seen as an act of adoration and glorification of God... and as the mystical reenactment of the Lord's sacrifice on the cross."

It is significant to note that before his ascent to the papal chair Cardinal Ratzinger publicly praised Fr. Gamber as "the one scholar who, among the army of pseudo liturgists, truly represents the liturgical thinking of the centre of the Church."

It is for reason that Benedict XVI today is attempting to resurrect the Old Rite through his *Moto Proprio* of September 14, 2007, since his objective is to restore confidence in the one liturgical remedy that has proven itself through the ages. St. Paul agrees: "Prove all things; hold fast that which is good." (1 Thessalonians 5:21) In his document on the Latin Mass issued April 30, 2011, the pope accentuates this very point: "What was sacred for prior generations remains sacred and great for us as well." (Universae Ecclesia)

Council Not Infallible

The pope while a cardinal had also stated that Vatican II is not infallible, and basically put the Council in its place when speaking to the bishops of Chile in 1988: "The truth is that this particular Council defined no dogma at all, and deliberately chose to remain on a modest level, as a merely pastoral council; and yet many treat it as though it had made itself into a sort of super-dogma which takes away the importance of all the rest." *(Cardinal Ratzinger on Vatican II)*

Pope Paul VI also cited the non-infallible status of Vatican II when he said that the Council "avoided issuing solemn dogmatic definitions backed by the Church's infallible teaching authority." (Speaking at the general audience, December 1, 1966)

Consider again his statement from 1970: "In many areas the Council has not so far given us peace but rather stirred up troubles and problems that in no way serve to strengthen the Kingdom of God within the Church or within its souls."

Such a statement could never be said of the Council of Trent or any previous council of Church history. The Mass of the Council of Trent has been called *the Mass that will never die* and has been the glory of the saints down through the centuries. Benedict XVI himself extolled the Old Mass in his historic document of July 7, 2007:

"It is known, in fact, that the Latin Liturgy of the Church... has been a spur to the spiritual life of many saints." *(Pope Benedict XVI, Summorum Pontificum)*

The Lady's Man Behind The Documents

To give us a better understanding of Vatican II, it is worth mentioning briefly Fr. Karl Rahner, a theological *peritus* (expert) and celebrated Rhine group member who was a central figure in the development of the Second Vatican Council, especially in the drafting of its documents. According to Fr. Ralph Wiltgen, who had arranged the Council's media coverage and who had interviewed thousands of clergy and bishops, Rahner was at the eye of this conciliar hurricane that was roaring against the Faith. Aside from being a "suspect theologian" who had implicitly denied the dogma of original sin, who sneered at priestly celibacy, and who dismissed the decrees of the Council of Trent as the inventions of a bigoted "sect", Rahner had been dating a steady girlfriend named Luise Rinser, a feminist and pro-abortion advocate serving as a reporter at Vatican II who had occupied his affections throughout the entirety of the Council.

The National Catholic Reporter ran a story on this late in 1997, which was based on the work of Pamela Kirk, an associate professor at St. John's University in Jamaica, New York, who is known as a Rahner specialist. Concerning their romance, Kirk writes: "Rinser was first brought to my attention in 1995 because of the publication of her letters to Karl Rahner, which revealed Rahner's passionate attachment to her."

According to first hand witnesses, Rinser was the central *figure* of Rahner's life at the time of the Council, during which he had sent her 758 love letters and had been in touch with her on a daily basis with frequent visits to her apartment, etc. His relation with her that began in 1962 would continue non-stop until 1984, with a total of 2, 203 letters that he had written her.

His obsession over her led him to become insanely jealous when she started turning her attention to a Benedictine abbot known as "M.A.", for which reason he began accusing her and succumbing to his wretchedness.

The point being, that this was the obsession that ravished his heart and perverted his judgment at a time when he was at the helm directing the course of the Second Vatican Council. According to Father Wiltgen, Rahner was revered by the entire Council at the recommendation of the Rhine group, which esteemed him as one of their most prized members-their protégé. As Wiltgen states, "Since the position of the German-language bishops was regularly adopted by the European alliance, and since the alliance position was generally adopted by the Council, a single theologian might have his views accepted by the whole Council if they had been accepted by the German-speaking bishops. There was such a theologian: Father Karl Rahner, S.J." (The Rhine Flows Into the Tiber)

What we see in Fr. Rahner is the advance of progressivist, anti-Catholic theology under the tag of Catholicism, which apparently was enhanced by his relationship with Rinser. The London Times wrote of her upon her death: "She remained a practicing Roman Catholic to the end of her days, but campaigned for abortion and against celibacy, as well as against the power of the priesthood." The German-American Institute also referred to Rinser as "a feminist, an environmentalist, and a protestor against atomic weapons."

But the fact that Fr. Rahner would even entertain a girlfriend tells the whole story. The priestly vows made at ordination strictly forbid a priest from having familiar relationships with women, but as with everything else, Fr. Rahner broke the rules and followed his own will. It fulfills St. Paul's prophecy concerning the false teachers of the last times who "resist the truth, men corrupted in mind, reprobate concerning the faith" who "lead captive silly women laden with sins" who are "incontinent, unmerciful, without kindness, traitors, stubborn, puffed up, and lovers of pleasures more than of God." (2 Timothy 3:3, 4, 6, 8)

The Bible says, "From the garments cometh a moth, and from a woman the iniquity of a man." (Ecc: 42:13) And the iniquity of Fr. Rahner, enhanced by his illicit connections, was the moving force behind his work at Vatican II. The documents certainly bear his fingerprints and have wrought irreparable damage throughout the Universal Church. "The gale force from Vatican II that uprooted dogma, dislodged morals, blew apart revered Catholic customs, destroyed Catholic landscapes, swept away Catholic landmarks, and toppled the entire Catholic edifice, could rightly be called "Hurricane Karl." *(John Venari, Catholic Family News)*

But this storm had its beginning in the dark seas of Teilhardism. Rahner was deeply imbued with the intellectual psychosis of Chardin who maintained that God and mankind are evolving together as one embryonic entity that will one day hatch and become a living host (see chapter 11). Chardin was condemned for his false academics in 1962, yet Rahner and the Council *periti* had the dare to pass his plagues on to the faithful. As an example of Rahner's deep and out-of-touch subjectivity, we cite the following quote from him:

"We are human beings only within humanity."

This falsely implies that we can potentially exist as something else outside of humanity, and that our present humanity is only the initial stage to being that something else, out of which we will eventually grow, evolve, and transform, so that we can one day be that something else in full [god], knowing good and evil. (Genesis 3:5) What we see here is the evolution of Chardin coming through the pen of Rahner.

The truth is that man will [13]always be what God created him to be, namely, the creature of man. In Heaven man assumes a sanctified state without a body, yes, but he nonetheless remains the same creature, known as man, who is called to live in eternal bliss with the Creator. The peoples in Heaven are known as the communion of saints, who are creatures, not gods. The Church Triumphant then is humanity in its ultimate state of realization!

But mankind can only arrive at that blissful state by renouncing the influence of the world and keeping himself united to God, most especially through the Mass and Rosary. The apostle Peter exhorts us to keep ourselves as "strangers and pilgrims" in this world, for we truly are as strangers passing through a country whose ways and language we know not. Our baptism calls us to depart the world and press toward the everlasting Kingdom without looking for acknowledgment along the way. St. John says, "Love not the world, nor the things which are in the world. If any man love the world, the love of the Father is not in him." (1 John 2:15)

But Rahner had his own idea about salvation. Like Luther, he discounted the reality of sin and its consequences, refusing responsibility for his actions, which is the truest sign of a guilty conscience. He believed that the whole world is evolving toward salvation, not just Catholics, and invented the idea that pagans and non Christians are just "anonymous Christians" who are also destined for salvation through their own inherent virtue, which in his estimation is their pride and their activity in the cult of man. Our calling to sanctify ourselves and to reject the temptation of

---

13 *Even Christ Himself, the Maker of the world, retains His humanity in the next world, since it is dogmatically taught that He is True God and True Man. And whereas His humanity now exists in its sublime and exalted state, He nonetheless retains His humanity as the representative of the human race who perpetually pleads our cause before the Father. Were it otherwise, we would not be able to receive His actual Body and Blood each day at Mass, which "is meat indeed: and… drink indeed." (John 6: 56)*

the world (original sin) was not something that Rahner wished to think about, since temptation is what guided him. He was seduced by his pride and his need to experience the "forbidden fruit," even defining love as "the light of knowledge." Did it not occur to him that true love is to give up any such knowledge or pseudo mysticism, and to "deny oneself?"

In a crucial essay in 1971, he writes: "In the unity of the experience of God and the experience of one's self, on the one hand, and in the unity of the experience of the self and encounter with the neighbor, on the other hand, we see that these three experiences are fundamentally one experience... God, self, community."

What Rahner here is saying is that the community of man is God, and that by uniting with the world of man we are uniting with God. But this is false. Union with God is what sets man apart from the world, since God is a separate and superior being whose "Kingdom is not of this world." (John 18: 36) Rahner fails to distinguish between the creature and the Creator, maintaining that God, self, and community are the same experience. This is the secular humanism we see so deeply engraved in the Vatican II documents, through which the emphasis today is on encounter with 'one another and the community.'

But what was the ink used to inscribe this error into the Council documents, but the iniquity of Rahner and his cohorts who refused to accept the absolute and omnipotent nature of the Creator who founded his Church as a Divine Monarchy, not a democracy. With Rahner, doctrine had to be arrived at through vote and consensus, with the other religions forming part of this democratic body. The idea of simply receiving the law out of God's hands (through the Council of Trent) was an abomination to Rahner. Like Lucifer he said, "I will not serve, I will not bow to thee." Yet, he and his clique were at the controls at Vatican II.

(Contributing sources: Fr. Karl Rahner-Heresy and Amor, John Venari; Karl Rahner SJ: A Theologian for the Twenty-First Century, Fr. Leo O'Donovan)

Religious Liberty

Religious liberty is that special endowment we all have to freely serve God without the interference of tyrannies or world councils that coerce us into adopting anything contrary to Church Tradition. Such was the way of the saints who freely abandoned themselves to God with complete immunity to all things so that they were answerable only to God without respect to persons. (Ephesians 6:6) In so doing they manifested perfect obedience to their superiors and to all the rules and regulations laid down by the Church in keeping with the Lord's instruction: "If you love Me, keep My Commandments." (John 14:15)

Religious liberty then is the freedom to obey God from the heart that we may be liberated from the curse of disobedience. It is that exclusive right we have as baptized Catholics to worship God in peace and liberty without the harassment of modernists who wish to impose a new religion upon man which the God of love had not given them to abide in.

But since Vatican II we see a new religious liberty entertained that advocates the rights of man, as if modern man has grown up and become a little god in a "brave new world" where he can think for himself without the guidance of a divine chaperone. We see this arrogant mentality encouraged right in the opening paragraph of *Dignitatis Humanae,* which is the Vatican II document on Religious Liberty:

"A sense of the dignity of the human person has been impressing itself more and more deeply on the consciousness of contemporary man, and the demand is increasingly made that men should act on their own

judgment." [1] *Again we read:* **"God has regard for the dignity of the human person whom He Himself created and man is to be guided by his own judgment and he is to enjoy freedom." [11]**

Here we see the Council honoring man's prerogative to be his own guide, which is contrary to the Creator. "For God will not except any man's person, neither will He stand in awe of any man's greatness: for He made the little and the great, and he has equally care for all." (Wisdom 6:8) Man's true dignity consists in his being made to the image of God, but this dignity is preserved by keeping one's innocence and yielding his judgment up to God, so that he makes God's judgment his own in matters of faith and morals. What God requires of us is a childlike submission to doctrine and Tradition as taught by the Savior Himself: "Unless you be converted, and become as little children, you shall not enter into the Kingdom of Heaven." (Matthew 18:3)

But according to the document, the Church may not infringe upon one's personal rights by laying down the law as to what they must do to be saved. It affirms the natural rights of man in matters of religion (Masonic freedoms), which is contrary to the previous papal teachings which deny any such rights. Pius IX in his Encyclical "Quanta Cura", Leo XIII in his Encyclicals "Libertas Praestantissimum" and "Immortale Dei" and Pius XII in his allocution "Ci Riesce" all affirm that there is no logical or scriptural basis for this humanist notion of human dignity, yet Vatican II seems to assert it as dogma.

The gist of the Religious Liberty document is to say that if a person's "moral conscience" leads them to adopt this or that formula for life even if it means renouncing the Faith and adhering to another religion, then that is their religious liberty which no man may oppose. This argument is founded not on the laws of God but on the "sacred rights" of man which, according to the document, must be honored at all cost.

However, we have to make a clear distinction between moral conscience and temptation. Moral conscience, of course, will always compel one to fear God and keep his Commandments which are already engraved "in the fleshy tablets of the heart." (2 Cor. 3:3) Whereas temptation will always lead one to depart the Commandments and follow his own will or sense of liberty where he doesn't allow God to hold the reins in his life as a Divine Monarch. Such liberty offends God and chains us to the shackles of guilt, which is no liberty. (John 8:34) There is no such thing as "my moral conscience told me to sin and be a rebel," for such is the manifestation of a guilty conscience, not a moral conscience. When God speaks man must listen and take heed of the Commandments, for He has granted man no license to resist the ordinance from On High.

It is true that man has been given a free will to choose between good and evil which God does not interfere with, since our eternal friendship with God must be a free will offering which is grounded in charity and not coercion. However, the abuse of our free will to choose evil is not honored by God nor is it permitted in the Church, nor is it a form of religious liberty. Man is granted the right to do what is right so that he can be liberated from wrong, and in this consists his religious liberty.

We might consider, too, that when Christ spoke to the people of His day He never once respected human opinion or personal liberty but laid down the truth as the absolute rule of life to follow if they wished to be saved. And whereas He did not force His doctrine upon the people and in fact allowed the people to oppose Him even unto His death on the cross, He nonetheless censured the people for their hypocrisy and never once pacified their defiled conscience by allowing them to feel right about what they were doing, since what they were doing was wrong. And He made sure they knew that! So this same sense of authority should be reflected by the Catholic hierarchy, since Christ has enjoined them with the office of the correction of others.

Yet the document forbids that the Church should enforce a universal rule of law upon its people as if Almighty God had no right to regulate the conduct of men within his own household! According to the document, mere man has the liberty to follow his 'moral conscience' but the Almighty has no liberty to govern His Church. What is fostered is the typical protestant argument that says "I can think for myself, I don't need a Church telling me what to do, I don't have to confess to a priest, I can find my own way directly to God, etc." This is the mentality that has separated a great many from the friendship of God through which they were banished to the fires of eternity, yet this is the very attitude defended in the Religious Liberty document of the Second Vatican Council.

With every liberal proposal of the document(s) there is an apparent conservatism (ambiguous double meaning) to cover its tracks so that under the pretext of honoring the rights of every human to freely adore his Creator, the document actually advocates that man has the liberty to follow his own licentious will:

"In all his activity a man is bound to follow his conscience... It follows that he is not to be forced to act in manner contrary to his conscience. Nor, on the other hand, is he to be restrained from acting in accordance with his conscience, especially in matters religious. The reason is that the exercise of religion, of its very nature, consists before all else in those internal, voluntary and free acts whereby man sets the course of his life directly to God." [3]

Here conscience is used interchangeably with self will so that on the surface it looks very honorable and says the truth that no man or religious authority may infringe upon the God given rights of men to direct themselves to God. But what the document is really saying is that the Church must honor the judgment of man to choose and decide for himself what course he is going to take, even if it means denying Christ. We might almost see the document as a pro-choice document, since what is honored is not the right choice but the "right" or "freedom" to choose, so that whatever choice is made is automatically honored by the Council.

For baptized Catholics their religious liberty consists in following the format that has already been laid out and chosen for them by the Church so that their only recourse as Catholics is to either embrace or reject it. The faithful are not given the liberty to introduce their own format to the Church or to adopt their own ideas, practices, doctrine or styles of dress (immodest) they may want to follow, unless it be derived from the Church. But according to Vatican II, the Church may not infringe upon their "moral conscience" to practice this religious liberty.

What is absurd is how the document cites our "human dignity" as the justification for this religious liberty. "The declaration of this Vatican Council on the right of man to religious freedom has its foundation in the dignity of the person, whose exigencies have come to be fully known to human reason through centuries of experience." [9] Since when is man's 'dignity' flaunted before the throne of God? What the Church issues in the way of documents or decrees must always have its foundation in the laws of God, not in the dignity of man.

The same applies for government. In any true Christian government the basic laws of God must always have bearing upon its judicial and legislative decisions which the people in turn must follow. Yet the Vatican II document states:

"It follows that a wrong is done when government [14]imposes upon its people, by force or fear or other means, the profession or repudiation of any religion." [6]

14　*Here again the document through ambiguous wording feigns to defend the people from the evil of coercive oppression when what it's really doing is preventing Christianity from reigning. It sees the mandates of moral authority as some sort of oppression that man must be guaranteed immunity from.*

Government indeed cannot force its people to profess a certain denomination, but it most certainly can profess Christianity to be the law of the land where the people at least are required to profess it in action through their compliance. But according to the Council, the U.S. Supreme Court did wrong in 1892 by declaring the United States to be "A Christian nation" in which "Our laws and our institutions must necessarily be based upon and embody the teachings of the Redeemer of mankind." The U.S. traditionally imposes the rule of Christianity as the law of the land to be obeyed by its citizens, namely, *thou shalt not kill, thou shalt not steal, thou shalt not rape, fornicate or abuse little children, etc.,* yet the Council seems to regard this mandatory compliance as 'coercion.' Does government not have a right and duty to enforce law and order?

According to the document religious zealots and terrorists should be free from such government coercion. "The freedom or immunity from coercion in matters religious which is the endowment of persons as individuals is also to be recognized as [15] their right." [4] Since when do people have a right to offend? If a person's religion dictates that he can murder Christians for Allah and crash his jet into the local skyscraper shall he now be immune from government censure or coercion? God forbid!

The fact that someone has a religious conviction doesn't make it right. With great liberty and conviction the Jews condemned Jesus to death in the name of "God their father," but Jesus told them who their father was, the devil, just as the devil is

---

15 *Which means it is their right to be free from the Council, whereas the dictates of moral authority should never be seen as coercion or something that man has a right to immunity from. The Council even admits that such rights are not affirmed by Scripture: "Revelation does not indeed affirm in so many words the right of man to immunity from external coercion in matters religious." (9) It is for reason that these so-called rights are not affirmed by revelation, since Holy Scripture would never encourage Christians to be immune to the laws of God.*

the father of those who suggest we may break the laws of God in view of religious liberty.

The great scandal bewitching modern man is this issue of human rights through which a major segment of humanity is now on the path to perdition. Unfortunately, the Religious Liberty document of Vatican II was a major foundation block for this new licentious order that has all but replaced the rule of Christianity that was once the hallmark of our society. Slowly but surely, the curse of human rights and relativism has overtaken the western psyche where people today strut about in their arrogance declaring their so-called "rights" to offend and to engage in lewd or alternative lifestyles, with much of this today being tolerated and even promoted by the Church! We see women today going up to Communion half naked with their indecency exposed, and in some cases even tattooed, yet not a word is uttered against this because it violates their "religious liberty."

With its pacifist theme, Vatican II compares to the French Revolution in that it too instructed the elders of the people to "let them eat cake" and to have their "religious liberty" instead of bringing them the spiritual meat and potatoes that is needed for their salvation. The end result has been a new order of spiritual anarchy where "the people" have taken the law into their own hands and have overrun the sanctuary with all manner of sham religious activity that has left the Church today in shambles.

Perhaps the most passionate opponent of the Religious Liberty document was Archbishop Marcel Lefebvre who warned of its detrimental consequences for the future, citing that it advocated "the right to cause scandal." He warned that with this document "a civil society endowed with Catholic legislation shall no longer exist" and said it would bring about "the disappearance in the Church of the missionary spirit for the conversion of souls." *(Bernard Tissiers, The Biography of Marcel Lefebvre)*

On June 29, 1976, the Archbishop also had this to say: "This right to religious freedom is blasphemous, for it attributes to God purposes that destroy His Majesty, His Glory, His Kingship. This right implies freedom of conscience, freedom of thought, and all the Masonic freedoms."

According to Lefebvre, the most incriminating evidence against the Religious Liberty of Vatican II was the enthusiastic support it received from the synagogue of satan. Consider the following from the Archbishop:

"This very year [1965], Yves Marsaudon, the Freemason, has published the book *L' oecumenisme vu par un franc-macon de tradition* (Ecumenism as Seen by a Traditional Freemason). In it the author expresses the hope of Freemasons that our Council will solemnly proclaim religious liberty... What further evidence do we need?"

Can we not understand why Pope Paul VI declared that "from some fissure the smoke of satan entered into the temple of God?" It is Lucifer who promotes the breaking of God's Commandments and it was his agents who gained control of the drafting apparatus at the Council which enabled them to draft up the blueprint for this new religious order. The document on Religious Liberty was like a battery to charge up the spirit of liberty at the Council and to encourage the endorsement of other religions (see following chapter), for which reason several of the cardinals did not want to sign it at its conclusion. But unfortunately, their *true* moral conscience was violated when they were told by the Council elite that if they didn't sign it they would not go on record as having participated at the Second Vatican Council.

It is for reason that Pope Paul VI stated the following in his speech at the end of Vatican II: "Profane and secular humanism has revealed itself in its terrible, anticlerical stature, and in one sense has defied the Council. The religion of God made man has met the religion of man who makes himself God." (December 7, 1965)

The pope here speaks of revolution in the Church. Cardinal Ratzinger actually admitted back in the 80s that the Vatican II document, *Gaudium et Spes* (in conjunction with the documents on Religious Liberty and Ecumenism), was intended to counteract the *Syllabus of Errors* by Pius IX and to set in motion the licentious principles of the French Revolution of 1789. "We might say that it is a revision of the Syllabus of Pius IX, a kind of counter-syllabus... Let us be content to say that the text serves as a counter-syllabus and, as such, represents, on the part of the Church, an attempt at an official reconciliation with the new era inaugurated in 1789." *(Cardinal Ratzinger, Principles of Catholic Theology, pp. 381-382, Ignatius Press, 1987)*

To think that the precepts of the French Revolution should be adopted by the Vatican Council! Is it any wonder why the Church has revolted from its past? What we see today is a *new order* of spiritual bondage where the people are forced to labor for this Masonic pyramid bearing the inscription *Novus Ordo Seclorum*. As they say, "we're building community; we're building up the temple of God." Fifty years of modernist oppression has kept the people in chains and has violated their Religious Liberty to sacrifice freely to God, only because these Pharaos of innovation have imposed these liturgical shackles and have sought to make the faithful immune to the laws of the Most High.

In conclusion, Religious Liberty is our exclusive right as Roman Catholics to continue in the Tradition of the Faith without being tainted with any stigma of modern reform, since our baptism gives us that right and duty to remain clean from elements foreign to the Faith. It is therefore incumbent upon the clergy to ensure that these sacred rights from God are not infringed upon by those who seek to depart the laws of God under the pretext of moral conscience.

Ecumenism

A key feature of the Second Vatican Council was its endorsement of other religions where the different churches of earth are treated as different branches of the same Universal Church. Consider the following from Vatican II Canon 844:

"Christ's faithful, for whom it is physically or morally impossible to approach a Catholic minister, may lawfully receive the sacraments of penance, the Eucharist and anointing of the sick from non-Catholic ministers in whose [16]Churches these sacraments are valid."

Here the Council validates the sacraments of non-Catholic churches which suggests heresy, since "non-Catholic" generally refers to protestant or man-made churches outside the Apostolic Faith. What is reflected here is a quest for unity with other religions which was a priority of the Second Vatican Council, as expressed in the opening section of *Unitatis Redintegratio,* the Council document on Ecumenism*:*

"The restoration of unity among all Christians is one of the principal concerns of the Second Vatican Council. Christ the Lord founded one Church and one Church only. However, many Christian communions present themselves to men as the true inheritors of Jesus Christ; all indeed profess to be followers of the Lord but differ in mind and go their different ways." [UR—1]

---

16 *This could hardly refer to Eastern Orthodox Churches since they're seldom referred to as "non-Catholic." According to Cardinal Ottaviani, the Eastern Orthodox churches were not supported by Vatican II.*

To propose a restorative solution to the present disunity it is first necessary to know its cause, which is no mystery. The reformers of the sixteenth century rejected Church teaching and broke away from Christ's institution giving rise to various sects and religious bodies which account for the present day segmentation of churches. So the solution is for separated brethren to renounce the errors of their protest and convert to the Church of Rome whereby they can have unity with the One True Church.

To preach that we should join other religions for the cause of Christian unity implies heresy, since it suggests that the world body of churches is the True Universal Church that is simply suffering from internal unity problems which can be solved by a mutual and compromising collaboration of its members. The solution, of course, is for separated brethren to leave their particular religions and adhere to the Catholic Church through which they have Christian unity. Pope Pius XII defined clearly who the true members of Christ are:

"Only those are to be included as members of the Church who have been baptized and profess the true faith, and who have not been so unfortunate as to separate themselves from the unity of the Body, or been excluded by legitimate authority for grave faults committed." (Pope Pius XII, Mystici Corporis)

For the record it's expedient to highlight the Church's dogmatic teaching on salvation so that there remains no question as to the Church's position on other religions. The following constitutes the Catholic Church's official decree on salvation:

"There is one holy Catholic and Apostolic Church, outside of which there is neither salvation nor remission of sins"
—Papal Bull, Pope Boniface VIII

The foregoing is a dogmatic decree that must be believed by the faithful which means it may never be questioned, altered or abrogated even by the pope, but must be firmly adhered to as the Church has understood and proclaimed it through the centuries. The same applies for all the Church's dogmatic decrees (e.g. Immaculate Conception, Transubstantiation, Primacy of the Pope, etc.) that carry that mark of infallibility.

Yet, Catholics today are under the illusion that Vatican II somehow superseded the past and canceled our allegiance to the former decrees. The conciliar documents have certainly contributed to this. Some in fact are heretical and constitute a denial of Church teaching. For instance it says in Unitatis Redintegratio:

"In certain circumstances, such as in prayer services "for unity" and during ecumenical gatherings, it is allowable, indeed desirable that Catholics should join in prayer with their separated brethren."

This new teaching endorses other religions and defies the Church's 2000 year prohibition against false worship as taught by the holy evangelist: "If any man come to you, and bring not this doctrine, receive him not into the house nor say to him, God speed you. For he that says to him, God speed you, communicates with his wicked works." (2 John 1:10, 11)

The Bible also says: "A man that is a heretic, after the first and second admonition, avoid." (Titus 3:10) Yet, Vatican II advocates that we have dialogue with such individuals and groups so that we can reconcile our differences. "Thus the way will be opened whereby this kind of "fraternal rivalry" will incite all to a deeper realization and a clearer expression of the unfathomable riches of Christ." (UR-11)

Since when does dialogue and consultation with schismatics bring us to "a deeper realization and a clearer expression of the unfathomable riches of Christ?" Jesus Christ Himself teaches the world and brings us His unfathomable riches through His Catholic Church and has no need of any man or religion to assist Him. The King of kings abides in his own palace and does not work through the temples of strangers. Yet Unitatis Redintegratio states:

"The Holy Spirit does not refuse to make use of other religions as a means of salvation."

This contradicts the Church's dogma that the Holy Spirit works only through the Catholic Religion outside of which there exists no salvation (extra ecclesiam nulla salus). Here we see a false ecumenism aimed at gaining the applause of other religious groups, and not their salvation. It is for reason that Archbishop Lefebvre refuted this error at the Council, saying, "There exists a spirit of non-Catholic or rationalist ecumenism that has become a battering ram for unknown hands to pervert doctrine."

True ecumenism is when we extend the beauties and riches of the Catholic Faith to the world without compromise so that all religions will stand back in awe and leave their particular religion and be joined to the Catholic Church.

But to achieve this, the clergy must return to the rule of discipline established through tradition. The crew on Peter's ship must resume their fishing out in the deep away from the secular coasts and let their nets down in traditional fashion, trusting that the Master will bring up a miraculous catch. (Luke 5:5-7) They must have firm footing up on deck with their gear and equipment and with a firm sense of detachment, and not look for human acceptance, embrace, or any sense of reward from their catch. Their only objective is to pull the fish on deck for Christ, because if they wade into the murky waters and meet them half way on their terms, it is the sharks that will catch them! Sadly, many bishops today are caught in the jaws of their enemies who flatter them with sweet words of ecumenical unity.

We saw this at the Council. There was a give and take treaty in force (1962) where the Soviets in attendance deceived the

Council and made like they were open to Church teaching, but where is the progress? Where is the conversion of Russia? Has Moscow received any overtures from Rome? No! The same applies with the Jewish synagogue and other groups that are beaming over the new Vatican policies of appeasement, but where are the fruits?

Because of 'ecumenism' the evangelical progress since the Council has all but ceased so that Marian and traditional groups have had to keep this evangelization going. The Church no longer thinks in terms of extending the Catholic religion to all peoples with the view that this is necessary for their salvation; it doesn't entreat them to "taste and see that the Lord is sweet." (Psalm 33:9)

It rather has adopted elements of Protestantism into its teaching, especially with respect to punishment for sin. The knowledge of hell and purgatory has virtually been eliminated today and replaced with the pacifist delusion that we're automatically forgiven through the mercy of God without penance and good works.

But this all ties back to [17]Martin Luther, the depraved reformist, who founded the protestant religion on the false premise that Christ died on the Cross to dispense with our obligations to God (Ten Commandments) so that we may sin licentiously without worry. Consider his famous quote from August of 1521:

---

17 *Dubbed the "spiritual ancestor of Hitler" by some, he was anti-Semitic and advocated murder in several of his writings. Consider the following quote from Luther: "To kill a peasant is not murder; it is helping to extinguish the conflagration. Let there be no half measures! Crush them! Cut their throats! Transfix them!... An insurgent is not worthy of being answered with reason, for he cannot understand it; such mouths must be stopped with fisticuffs till their noses bleed... Startle their ears with bullets, and send their heads flying in the air... If they say I am very hard and merciless, mercy be damned. Let whoever can, stab, strangle, and kill them like mad dogs." (Erlangen Edition of Luther's works, vol. 24, p. 294)*

"Be a sinner and sin boldly, but believe and rejoice in Christ even more boldly . . . No sin will separate us from the Christ, even though we commit fornication and murder a thousand times a day." *(From Luther's famous letter to Philip Melanchthon, August 1, 1521, LW Vol. 48, pp. 281-2)*

Herein is the crux and foundation of Protestantism which asserts that [18]Jesus already paid the price so that our works will neither save nor condemn us. This is a devious lie with no scriptural basis which was rightfully condemned by the Council of Trent, yet Vatican II asserts that the Holy Spirit works through such a religion and even declares its liturgies and ceremonies to be the manifestation of God's workings within their institution:

"The brethren divided from us also carry out many liturgical actions of the Christian religion. In ways that vary according to the condition of each Church or community, these liturgical actions most certainly can truly engender a life of grace, and, one must say, can aptly give access to the communion of salvation. It follows that the separated Churches and communities . . . have been by no means deprived of significance and importance in the mystery of salvation. For the Spirit of Christ has not refrained from using them as a means of salvation." (UR-3)

According to Michael Davies, these perfidious texts and the ensuing "disease of ecumania" that spread throughout the Universal Church were the "direct result of the presence of Protestant observers at the Second Vatican Council." (Pope John's Council)

---

18 *This coincides closely with the Masonic plan to infiltrate the Council with the presumptuous fallacy about salvation as outlined in item no. 2 of their 34 guidelines issued in March 1962: "Put a stop to practice of penance during Lent, such as eating no meat on Fridays, or fasting. Halt any acts of self-denial. Replace by acts of joy, happiness and love of neighbor. Say that Christ already won Heaven for us, and that the efforts of humans are to no avail."*

Martin Luther

Luther preached that man doesn't need to appease God to be saved, arguing that Christ already did this for us, so that "no sin will separate us from the Christ, even though we commit fornication and murder a thousand times a day." His quirk about justification formed the very crux of the Protestant Reformation that swept half of Europe away from the Faith. He was condemned a heretic on June 15, 1520 and then excommunicated from the Church on January 3, 1521.

Meeting the demands of Luther is something that Rome today officially recognizes, as we read in the 1980 Joint Catholic-Lutheran Commission which grew out of Vatican II: "Among the ideas of the Second Vatican Council, we can see gathered together much of what Luther asked for, such as the following: description of the Church as 'The People of God' (a democratic and non hierarchic idea); accent on the priesthood of all baptized; the right of the individual to freedom of religion."

The Vatican's Joint Declaration of the Doctrine of Justification (posted on the Vatican website) also states the following in support of Luther: "For the Lutheran tradition, the doctrine of justification has retained its special status. Consequently it has also from the beginning occupied an important place in the official Lutheran-Roman Catholic dialogue."

PROTESTANT ADVISORY BOARD

As mentioned earlier, there were six known Protestant delegates at the Second Vatican Council who played a significant role in shaping the Council documents. Michael Davies confirms this in his book on the New Mass where he states that "six Protestant observers were invited to advise this Consilium. They played an active part in the preparation of the New Mass." Their names for the record were: Canon Jasper, Dr. McAfee Brown, Professor George Lindbeck, Professor Oscar Cullmann, Pastor Rodger Schutz, and Archdeacon Pawley.

Far from being mere observers, these delegates were actually acting as an advisory board to the Council. Monsignor Baum (later Cardinal Baum) in an interview with the Detroit News on June 27, 1967, commented on the role of these six Protestant participants: "They are not simply there as observers, but as consultants as well, and they participate fully in the discussions on Catholic liturgical renewal."

According to Archbishop Lefebvre, a key objective in having the observers present was to intimidate the Council from issuing anything that might offend separated brethren. This is confirmed by Dr. Moorman, head of the Anglican delegation at the Council, who noted that the observers "were providing some kind of check on what was being said. Every bishop who has stood up to speak has known that, in the tribune of S. Longinus was a group of intelligent and critical people, their pencils and biros poised to take down what he said and possibly use it in evidence against him and his colleagues on some future occasion... Members of the Council tended, therefore, to be very sensitive to what the representatives of those other communions were thinking, and did their best to avoid saying anything which was likely to cause offense. If some Father forgot himself and said things which were bound to cause a flutter in the observers' tribune, he was sometimes rebuked by some later speaker." *(Michael Davies, Pope John's Council)*

Aside from intimidating the Council, Dr. Moorman goes on to say that the observers were able to "make their views known at special weekly meetings of the Unity Secretariat (see below), and had personal contacts with the Council fathers." Professor Cullmann of the Lutheran Church summed it up on December 4, 1965: "The hopes of Protestants for Vatican II have not only been fulfilled, but... have gone far beyond what was believed possible." *(Xavier Rynne, The Fourth Session, 1966)*

The Protestant influence on the Council was greatly enhanced by the *Secretariat for the Promotion of Christian Unity* that was established on June 5, 1960. Its purpose was to establish relations with Christian bodies outside the Catholic Church and to invite their representatives to the Council.

Augustin Cardinal Bea, S.J., of the Rhine group was unfortunately appointed to head the Secretariat, who in turn made it a significant instrument of ecumenical exchange as well as a very powerful force within the Council. The Secretariat had the task of drafting the crucial schema on Ecumenism, discussed in this chapter, as well as to contribute to the texts for the decrees on Religious Liberty and on the Jews.

At a reception organized by the Unity Secretariat, Cardinal Bea boasted of the contribution made by the observers in formulating the Decree on Ecumenism, when he said: "I do not hesitate to assert that they have contributed in a decisive way to bringing about this result." Professor B. Mondin, of the Pontifical Propaganda College for the Missions, stated that observers such as Dr. Cullmann made "a valid contribution" to drawing up the Council documents.

That Vatican II was instrumental in renewing the principles of the Protestant Reformation in the Catholic Church is evidenced by the words of Fr. Edward Schillebeeckx, a prominent figure of the Council, when he remarked: "One is astonished to find oneself more in sympathy with the thinking of Christian, non-Catholic 'observers' than with the views of one's own brethren on the other side of the dividing line. The accusation of connivance with the Reformation is therefore not without foundation."

The accusation indeed is warranted. The thrust of Vatican II was its call for unity with world religions and goes so far as to say that if there exists a rift between the Catholic Church and other religions (because of its conviction to stand apart from these religions) then the Church is "failing to recognize its own catholicity."

But is it not rather the world that has failed to recognize the catholicity of the Roman Church outside of which there is no catholicity? The world's religions from the beginning have battered the One True Church without cause in the same way the Pharisees were driven with envy to batter the Christ without cause. These groupings through the ages have unleashed this same malice against the Church so that in every case without exception these rifts, ruptures and dissentions have been the fault of these religions which failed to recognize the goodness of the Creator emanating from the Church of Rome.

But not according to Vatican II. The conciliar document speaks of the divisions of the early Church:

"There arose certain rifts… but in subsequent centuries much more serious dissensions appeared and large communities became separated from full communion with the Catholic Church for which, often enough, men of both sides were to blame." [UR-3]

Here the Council blames the Church for much of this division which isn't surprising when we consider the psyche of the Council. According to Vatican II, the world with its various religions constitutes the True Universal Church and sees the Church of Rome as part of this universal body that has been creating disunity through the ages by its allegiance to dogma, and that the solution to this division is for the Church to discard these 'bigoted convictions' and consult with the other world religions that it might better learn to behave itself and merge with the rest as one.

But since when is unity with other religions a consideration? Christ said: "Do not think that I came to send peace upon earth: I came not to send peace, but the sword. For I came to set man at variance against his father, and the daughter against her mother, and the daughter in law against her mother in law." (Matthew 10:34, 35)

Lucifer, the prince of this world, has been generating this global movement that we all be one. The power of the devil operating through the internationalist elite has been working around the clock to unite all peoples and religions into an international one-world religion, a movement which the Second Vatican Council falsely attributes to the Holy Spirit:

"In recent times more than ever before, He [God] has been rousing divided Christians to remorse over their divisions and to a longing for unity. Everywhere large numbers have felt the impulse of this grace, and among our separated brethren also there increases from day to day the movement, fostered by the grace of the Holy Spirit, for the restoration of unity among all Christians. This movement toward unity is called "ecumenical". . . the one visible Church of God, a Church truly universal." [UR-2]

Note again the false definition of One Universal Church. With its theme of secular unity, Vatican II also attempts in a general way to redefine "communion" to no longer mean our communion with Christ in the Eucharist but a new-found communion with world religions. A great many of today's guidelines reflect this conciliar ideal and could very well have come from the Council documents as we see here in the U.S. Catholic Bishop's *Guidelines for the Reception of Communion:*

"We welcome our fellow Christians [separated brethren] to this celebration of the eucharist as our brothers and sisters. We pray that our common baptism and the action of the Holy Spirit in this eucharist will draw us closer to one another and begin to dispel the sad divisions that separate us. We pray that these will lessen and finally disappear, in keeping with Christ's prayer for us "that they may all be one." (John 17:21)

Note the twist on scripture that is used to advance a secular cause. Christ was praying that the Gentiles would hear the doctrine of His Apostles so that they too "may be one" with Him. The scriptural verse of John 17:21 references the Apostles' oneness with Christ, not their oneness with the world. Christ did not come to unite with the world or world religions but to call us out of the world that we may unite with him in his visible Kingdom whereby we have our catholicity. (John 18:36)

Those who leave the confines of the Universal Church renounce their catholicity and forfeit their salvation.

However, members of other religions [19]can sometimes be saved through the grace of the Catholic Church if they are not yet converted and are not harboring spiteful resistance against the One True Church. But these religions in themselves are void and incapable of producing one thread of grace or salvation for the simple reason that they are man-made, as opposed to the Roman Catholic Church which is the only religion on earth that was founded and given to the world by the Creator himself, who is Jesus Christ.

This is not to imply that members of other religions cannot aspire for a true unity with God since the grace of the Catholic Church will often reach into these gatherings, and like a magnet draw them upward that they might convert to the Church of Rome. These members indeed will often exhibit godly behavior (e.g. prolife work, almsgiving, etc.) but this virtue is due to their own merit and the Holy Spirit's prompting of their good works; it is not due in any way to their synagogue or religious blueprint which actually deters the good they are trying to do. The evangelical mission of the Church is to reach such persons and pull them through that they might convert fully to the Catholic Church, but Vatican II sustains their alienation from God by respecting their dead religion.

This is especially true with respect to the post-conciliar policy with the Jews. The Church's commission is to convert the Jews and bring them the true Manna from Heaven and not

---

19 *This is an undefined or ordinary teaching of the Catholic Church upheld by Pius XII and others known as Baptism of Desire. Members of other religions can sometimes be saved, but their salvation is through the Catholic Church and is not due to their religion. The mercy of God will overlook the ignorance of those who never heard the Gospel or received a proper presentation of it and sometimes will apply the merits of Christ to them in an extraordinary way if he sees they are innocent.*

be like the Nazis who refused to give them the bread from their own table. The Church traditionally had always extended them this royal invitation to come partake in the Lord's Supper *(e.g. Pius XII helped convert 800,000 Jews)*, but today they're being told to stay in their own prison camp and starve. In that sense the liberal hierarchy is more anti-Semitic than those whom they so label *(e.g. Bishop Williamson)* because they would rather watch the Jews suffer an eternal holocaust before witnessing for their Catholic Faith! Charity is not withholding the Kingdom of God from the Jews but charity means bringing "the unfathomable riches of Christ" to all peoples and returning to the Church's pre-conciliar policy with Jews and Gentiles with the understanding that these former policies were perfect charity in action.

Now concerning societies that worship idols, it could not be said that they adore the True God for the simple reason that they don't know the True God (collectively). For one cannot know God unless He first be known to him through revelation. (Romans 10:14) Those who bow to idols in ignorance are not necessarily guilty of idolatry and in many cases are truly intending to honor the Higher Power, but what is actually named or called upon in these cultures is not God but an imaginary figment produced by the devil. Yet the Vatican II document, *Nostra Aetate,* states:

"Muslims adore the one God, living and subsisting in Himself; merciful and all-powerful, the Creator of heaven and earth, who has spoken to men; they take pains to submit wholeheartedly to even His inscrutable decrees, just as Abraham, with whom the faith of Islam takes pleasure in linking itself, submitted to God... They value the moral life and worship God especially through prayer, almsgiving and fasting." [3]

Had the Council fathers forgotten that Christ is the Only True God that has spoken to men and that He does not abide in the temples of Baal? Had they forgotten the Quran's teaching that Jesus Christ is not the Son of God? Did they overlook the Islamic precept that anyone who is not a Muslim should be slain? Did they forget that Allah is an infernal idol and that Mohammad was his agent? Did they overlook the fact that Islam is under the powers of darkness and has been battering the Church of the "One God" since the sixth century?

What other religions do not realize is that Christ abides physically here on earth, but his physical presence is found only in the Church which he himself instituted (Tabernacle). Christ came to earth and established one institution of religion under the authority of Peter with the Sacrifice of the Mass being the very foundation of this institution. The Mass constitutes the very heartbeat of Christianity around which the entire Mystical Body revolves.

It is because other religions do not possess or celebrate the Holy Sacrifice in their communities (being cut off from apostolic succession) that they are invalid and incapable of imparting any grace of salvation to their members. Just as the body without the heart is dead so these religious bodies are dead with no circulatory grace because they are severed from the vine. What Christ said to his Apostles applies:

"As the branch cannot bear fruit of itself, unless it abide in the vine, so neither can you, unless you abide in Me. I am the vine; you the braches: he that abides in Me, and I in him, the same beareth much fruit: for without Me you can do nothing." (John 15: 4-6)

The various denominations outside the Church are at the mercy of Christ the King who reigns through his representative in Rome. The other religions can only be grafted to the vine on papal terms, yet Vatican II asserts that the Church must be grafted to the world churches on compromising terms which breaks the continuity with the past.

AND THIS BREAK WITH TRADITION is in fact what distinguishes Vatican II from the previous ecumenical councils of history. Advocates of the Council will argue that the Church's pre-conciliar teachings are incorporated in the Council documents, which is true. There are some orthodox precepts set forth here and there in the documents, but these holy precepts stand on their own merit without the Council and needn't be seen in relation to the Council. The danger with this is that the faithful stand a chance of seeing the old teachings now in a new light, which was one of the objectives of the reformers.

According to Archbishop Lefebvre, "The good texts have served as cover to get those texts which are snares, equivocal, and denuded of meaning, accepted and passed." *(I Accuse the Council, 1998)* Indeed, the display of orthodoxy and reform side by side worked to the enemy's advantage, since it served to sell the reform and to tempt the Church into thinking that the reform grew out of the Church's 2000 year tradition, which of course it didn't. The heresies of the past all occurred in the course of Church history, but that didn't make them part of Tradition.

What we have today is the heresy of Modernism which denies Tradition and maintains that the Church should change in order to keep up with the times, which was the theme of Vatican II progressivists. Right from go the plan was to dub the reform a 'renewal' or 'restoration' in order to conceal the fact that they were pressing toward something new. Their thinking was more in line with Chardin who was a major underlying force behind the modernist movement of the twentieth century.

Chardin vs. Tradition

Teilhard de Chardin

The influence of Teilhard de Chardin (1881-1955) has been overlooked and not given due consideration by the Church in our time. His work to integrate the evolution theory with Catholicism helped to spawn the modern day notion that the Catholic Church is an evolutionary reform process that goes through phases of change over time, which of course is false. Monkeys do not grow out of fish, people do not grow out of monkeys, and liberal reform does not grow out of tradition. What God has established from the beginning, whether spiritual or physical, remains, and does not change.

But not according to Chardin. He believed that God and the universe are evolving and pressing toward some glorious light or new Pentecost, an error that was applied at Vatican II. As he saw it, God is a cosmic entity that has yet to hatch and become a living host. According to Chardin, God and the Church are still growing and have yet to come into their full being. And even though his New Age lunacy was condemned by the Church in 1962, his ideas nonetheless underscored much of the thinking at the Council, which in turn has caused the Church in our time to evolve away from God, save the elect.

Can we understand now why Chardin is such a darling among today's progressives? His thinking was certainly in force at the Council, as Bishop Adrian relates: "The European periti, who really imposed their theories upon the bishops, were themselves deeply imbued with the errors of Teilhardism. . . which errors ultimately destroy all divine faith and morality and all constituted authority."

Teilhard's influence upon the Church goes beyond what most Catholics would ever care to realize. Even orthodox thinkers will sometimes adopt his weird ideas into their arguments, saying that the whole of Tradition has been an ongoing evolutionary reform, even citing the various revisions in the traditional calendar (which constituted no significant change), and that Vatican II is just part of the reform process, and that the way we follow Tradition is by following the Council.

Our allegiance to Tradition, of course, is not tied to the Council. Tradition is Tradition, and liberal reform is liberal reform, and the two are not connected. A true reform as God would see it is any wholesome, disciplinary measure that renews the Church and brings it back to its traditional roots *(e.g. Tridentine decrees, prayer to St. Michael after Mass, etc.)*. But in 1962 no such reform or restoration was needed, the Church's constitution was in perfect shape.

What was needed was a firm adherence to Tradition as expressed by St. Paul when exhorting the people of the last times: "Stand fast; and hold the traditions which you have learned, whether by word, or by our epistle." (2 Thess. 2:14) This was the Apostle's remedy for withstanding the "operation of error" that would test the world in the last days.

The popes of the previous century had warned against the errors of Modernism that were coming upon the Church. Pius X was particularly emphatic about not tailoring doctrine to suit the world. He understood that the most ecumenical thing that can be done to convert a changing world is to simply uphold the unchanging Tradition of the Faith. This is the formula that has stood the test of time; this is what attracts souls to God. He said, "The true friends of the people are neither revolutionaries nor innovators, but men of tradition."

But advocates of the conciliar reform still argued that we need to make the Faith more accessible to the people and reach the youth. But had they considered God's designs for the youth to be deficient? Did they not recognize that the Church's guidance before the Council was virtually perfect and that young people in former times were generally more pure, upright, studious, well intending, respectful of parents and authority and more apt to grow up and put aside adolescent snares at an early age? (1 Cor. 13:11) Can they not see rather that the Catholic youth of today are more disrespectful, disobedient, obsessed with forbidden enticements and generally led by temptation and "rock and roll" being spawned even by today's contemporary Masses which were supposedly designed to reach the youth?

Yea, has it not dawned on today's bishops that their procedures have been wrong? Can they not open their eyes and see that the Church today is carousing around a golden calf with the words "Vatican II" stamped on its rear hind?

The great tragedy of our time is that the hierarchy has lost confidence in what Christ left them through Tradition, where they feel they must look for new and exciting ways of worshiping God. The Church since the Council has been laboring all night in the dark with little success because its ministers haven't learned to take the Master at His word and let their nets down the traditional way. They've employed the invention of their own hands (innovation) and what have been the fruit of their labors but escalating divorce, immorality and a general departure from the everlasting ordinance, all done of course in the name of obedience. It is truly the masterstroke of the devil that has succeeded in sowing disobedience into the Church through obedience.

It's the story of Eve and the serpent again. The Church was called to be the Spouse of Christ without spot or blemish, but at the Council she became unruly and threw off her wedding veil and started flirting with other religions to the end that a general spirit of infidelity has set in, evidenced even by the way women no longer cover their heads in Church before God. The eternal mandates for women set forth in 1 Corinthians 11:5 are now treated as something outdated, as if today's woman is now exempt from the Commandments.

The Council advocated feminist rights and called for a greater role for women and laity in the Church, which of course is Marxist. Representatives from the Soviet Union were allowed to sit in on the Council and introduce revolutionary precepts of lay empowerment, as it was their aim to overthrow the Church's episcopal authority. This would eventually lead to the use of lay Eucharistic ministers and women lectors that have since undermined the Church's hierarchical structure. The ugly hand of Communism has truly reached in to desecrate the Body of Christ.

Communism / Infiltration

In 1917 the Blessed Virgin at Fatima warned that if Her requests to convert Russia were not heeded, the agents of Communism would later infiltrate the Church with their errors. Vatican II provided a perfect opening to accelerate the influx of Communists into the Church. The plan in 1962 was to invite the Soviets to the Second Vatican Council, which is why certain dissident cardinals met secretly in France beforehand to sign the infamous 1962 Moscow-Vatican Treaty with Archbishop Nikodim. Russia's objective was to subvert the Church through the Council, so it was crucial to their plan that the Church first be bound by a treaty that promised there would be no censure of Communism at the Council. Since 1962 the Church's hands and feet have been bound by this treaty while the agents of Communism have been gleefully at work dismantling the Church incognito.

Infiltration of Catholic Seminaries

Anatoliy Golitsyn was formerly a high-ranking KGB official involved in espionage and counter-espionage who defected to the United States in 1961. In 1985, Golitsyn reported that Russian Orthodox priests are controlled and directed by the KGB in order to promote cooperation between Soviet churches and Western Catholics to help establish a united front for disarmament and convergence (peace and justice movements). In 1990 Golitsyn warned against the Vatican's (1962) policy of appeasement with the Communist Party:

"The Vatican should reverse its mistaken support for the renewal of the KGB régimes. . . It fails to understand that greater apparent official tolerance of religion is accompanied by a secret drive to increase Party and KGB penetration of the Catholic and other churches and to use agents therein for political and strategic purposes. As part of the program to destroy religion from within, the KGB, in the late 1950s started sending dedicated young Communists to ecclesiastical academies and seminaries to train them as future church leaders. These young Communists joined the Church at the call of the Communist Party. . . to implement its general line [unchanged policy] in the struggle against religion."

Memoirs of a Communist Agent

Back in the 60s the memoirs of a KGB agent were discovered by a French nurse named Marie Carre while attending to an auto accident in which the agent was killed. In his briefcase was found a set of biographical notes which she kept and read, and then decided to publish because of their extraordinary content. The end result is a little book entitled, *AA 1025—The Memoirs of an Anti-Apostle,* which reveals the sentiments and plans of this Communist who had deliberately entered the priesthood (along with others) with the intention of destroying the Catholic Church from within. The following excerpt is taken from his notes:

"It was during those days that I launched on the market the program that would allow Catholics to be accepted by Protestants... I prophesied with assurance the suppression of Latin, of priestly vestments, of statues and images, of candles and prie-dieu (so that they could kneel no more). And I also started a very active campaign for the suppression of the Sign of the Cross. This Sign, and also genuflections, are all ridiculous customs. I also prophesied (and we were then in 1940) the disappearance of altars, replaced by a completely bare table, and also of all the crucifixes, in order that Christ be considered as a man, not as a God. I insisted that Mass be only a community meal, to which all would be invited, even unbelievers... I searched for the means of suppressing the Pope. I consoled myself by hoping that we would surely succeed in making him look foolish."

The agent's identity is not known, but is known only by a code number that was assigned to him by the Russian Secret Police, AA 1025, which means Anti-Apostle number 1025. There were 1024 similar agents that had gone before him, some of whom became bishops and who could have even penetrated to high positions within the Roman Curia. He himself participated at Vatican II and contributed to the formulation of ambiguous documents which laid the groundwork for destructive changes in the Church. The focal point of his attack, as with any true Communist, was the Holy Eucharist. Consider the following from his memoirs:

"To weaken more the notion of 'Real Presence' of Christ, all decorum will have to be set aside. No more costly embroidered vestments, no more music called sacred, especially no more Gregorian Chant, but a music in jazz style, no more sign of the Cross, no more genuflections, but only dignified stern attitudes. Moreover, the faithful will have to break themselves from the habit of kneeling, and this will be absolutely forbidden when receiving Communion.... Very soon, the Host will be laid in the hand in order that all notion of the Sacred be erased. In order to destroy all sacredness in the cult, the priest will be invited to say the whole Mass in vernacular [common language]."

The anonymous agent, as with countless others throughout the world, was obsessed with destroying the Faith, and he labored feverishly around the clock to formulate a plan on how to subvert the Catholic Church with change. To this end he committed his entire life to learning Catholic theology so as to gain inside access to masterfully communicate and pull the Catholic hierarchy away from their traditional roots. His plan was to make them feel ashamed of their catholicity by insisting that their 'bigoted convictions' have caused 'harm' to others throughout the world. Consider the following from his notes:

"At that time, I showed great energy to destroy the Marian cult. I insisted greatly upon the grief that Catholics and Orthodox sects caused to Protestants by keeping up their numerous devotions to the Virgin Mary. I pointed out that the dear separated brethren were more logical and wiser... I therefore advocated the suppression of the Rosary and of the numerous feast days reserved to Mary."

Communist Infiltration of the Catholic Hierarchy

Manning Johnson, a former official of the Communist Party in America, gave the following testimony in 1953 to the House Un-American Activities Committee:

"Once the tactic of infiltration of religious organizations was set by the Kremlin. . . the communists discovered that the destruction of religion could proceed much faster through the infiltration of the Church by communists operating within the Church itself. The communist leadership in the United States realized that the infiltration tactic in this country would have to adapt itself to American conditions and the religious makeup peculiar to this country. In the earliest stages it was determined that with only small forces available to them, it would be necessary to concentrate communist agents in the seminaries. The practical conclusion drawn by the Red leaders was that these institutions would make it possible for a small communist minority to influence the ideology of future clergymen in the paths conducive to communist purposes.... **The policy of infiltrating seminaries was successful beyond even our communist expectations."**

Back in the early 50s, Bella Dodd, a former high ranking official of the American Communist Party, testified before the House Un-American Activities Committee concerning the Communist infiltration of Church and State and provided detailed explanations of the Communist subversion of the Church. Speaking as a former insider in the know, she said: "In the 1930s we put eleven hundred men into the priesthood in order to destroy the Church from within." Twelve years before Vatican II, she said: "Right now they are in the highest places in the Church." She also predicted changes in the Church that would be so drastic that "you will not recognize the Catholic Church."

Bella's prophecy certainly has come to pass. The Church in our time is but a carcass of its former glory, stripped of all holiness and piety, because the fathers of the Council lent their ears to these Red agents who called for "change." Dodd describes their inside work of:

- Encouraging "the promotion of a pseudo-religion: something that resembled Catholicism but was not the real thing."

- Labeling "the *Church of the past* as being oppressive, authoritarian, full of prejudices, arrogant in claiming to be the sole possessor of truth, and responsible for the divisions of religious bodies throughout the centuries."

- Shaming Church leaders into "an 'openness to the world,' and to a more flexible attitude toward all religions and philosophies."

Because of their presence in the Church a spirit of terror prevails today where clergy are intimidated from upholding Tradition in all spheres of their ministry, especially the Mass, and from condemning the sins against the Sacraments that are rampant in most of our churches, especially the practice of Communion in the hand. Though the revolution of today is spiritual, it is nonetheless real and destructive, and has taken its toll.

Russia today continues with its plan to subdue the Church and the world, but their strategy at this time is to conceal this plan under the guise of a collapse of power. As they finalize their plan for world conquest they don't want the world to suspect what they're about to do (invade the west), so the *Bear* is simply playing dead while secretly promoting this global pacifism (green peace) that advocates the overthrow of the establishment.

In the Church, this pacifist delusion of the last times is manifest with the false security that *all* are forgiven and that a day of sunshine has dawned upon Christianity (New Pentecost). The agents of Communism infiltrated the Church with a plan to erase from our minds any notion of punishment or divine justice so that when this scourge (Russia) came upon society and the Church we would not be ready.

Communism of course is one of the tentacles of the internationalist octopus that is working around the clock to dissolve the institution of Christianity (papacy) and bring about a New World Order. The prospective vision of Vatican II was a new church of man with the unification of all religions, so the Council was an opening for this World Council of Churches to get in the door and use the Church as a forum to advance this new communistic order (Novus Ordo).

In his 1974 book, *Athanasius and the Church of Our Time*, Bishop Rudolph Graber quotes a prominent Freemason as saying: "The goal of Freemasonry is no longer the destruction

117

of the Church, but to make use of it by infiltrating it." This is exactly what has happened in our time. The pirates of One-World got at the helm and are driving the Faith shipwreck onto secular coasts.

If only the world had listened to Pope Paul's warning about satan in the Church! With all that has transpired in the past forty years it somehow hasn't dawned on the faithful that the ancient serpent reared its head at the Second Vatican Council and challenged the Faith to a dual. It was this very onslaught against the Faith that the Blessed Virgin sought to alert us to in Her Secret at Fatima.

The adversary's greatest victory came with the September 1964 instruction *Inter Oecumenici,* article 48, which eliminated the traditional prayer to St. Michael after Mass, this being perhaps the most destructive reform of the Council. This was in keeping with the Concilium which states that "elements" which "were added with but little advantage are now to be discarded." [article 50] The purpose of this document was to implement the norms of Vatican II as they originally planned it, with the suppression of the St. Michael prayer being first on their agenda.

This was to prove fatal for the Church. For it was through the restraining force of this great archangel that the influence of the devil was formerly held back through the ages and kept out of the Church (2 Thess. 2:6, 7), but by removing St. Michael this opened the door to infiltration and gave the enemy easy access to enter.

THE PLAN was to get at the controls and use the liturgy as a tiller to steer the Church in a new direction. For plans were in the works forty-nine years ago to turn the priest around and introduce modifications to the liturgy that would obscure the Church's doctrine and advance a new secular light not tied to holy Tradition (New Pentecost).

In so doing progressives were careful to promote the new changes in the pope's name in order to better sell it to the faithful. What had begun as a holy ecumenical Council had now become a think-tank of treachery and deceit. The fact that several of the Council fathers were entertaining birth control, religious liberty, and the discarding of the Primacy of Peter was a clear indication that fidelity to the Faith was not a priority at the Council. Consider this declaration from Vatican II Canon 336:

"This College of Bishops, in which the apostolic body abides in an unbroken manner, is, in union with its head and never without this head, also the subject of supreme and full power over the universal Church."

Here the Council audaciously declares the college of bishops to be equal to the pope, which is heretical. The pope alone possesses supreme power to govern the Church, since he is the Vicar of Christ who directs the entire college of bishops as their superior. The secondary authority of the bishops over the flock derives strictly from their subordination to the pope, without which they have no authority. Whereas the pope possesses full authority over the Church without the consent of the bishops. If the bishops disobey the pope, the faithful are not obliged to obey them, but if the pope disregards the bishops the faithful must still obey the pope. Having supreme power is what enables to pope to command the bishops, yet the bishops have no power (legal power) to command the pope or to oppose him. Therefore it is erroneous to say that the bishops are "also the subject of supreme and full power over the universal Church", since it is a power they do not have.

This challenge of the Holy Father's authority defies the Primacy of Peter (dogma) and was the very foundation of the spiritual revolt that usurped the Second Vatican Council. According to Pope Paul VI, the Church since the Council is on a path of self destruction. "The Church finds herself in an hour of anxiety, a disturbed period of self-criticism, or what would even be better called self-destruction. It is an interior revolution, acute, and complicated, which nobody expected after the Council. It is almost as if the Church were attacking itself." (December 7, 1968 in his address at Lombardi Seminary)

It is significant to note that of the 21 ecumenical councils of Church history Vatican II was the first council that invited participating members who were not in strict union with the Church, including those that were Protestant and Jew. It was precisely this influx of outsiders that infected the Church's immune system when dissident members of the Curia began adopting their ideas for the Mass and Sacraments.

However, this infection didn't automatically mushroom into a global virus in 1965. The seeds of error were quietly embedded in the Council and then watered with the new liturgy that was implemented in 1969, so that what has sprouted forth in our time is everything planned by this sinister coalition from the beginning, namely, the guitar Mass, the indecent dress, Communion in the hand, lay ministers, women speakers, openness to other religions, the denial of purgatory and hell, the practice of spiritism and sorcery, the charismatic renewal, etc.

Conspiracy

At the levers behind the scene were the members of the Masonic P.2 Lodge working through their affiliate members in the clergy. Of particular mention again is the infamous Annibale Bugnini who was master architect of the New Mass. Consider item no. 11 from their 34 guidelines issued in March 1962 for the destruction of the Catholic Church:

"Stop the practice of saying Mass before the Holy Eucharist in the tabernacle. Do not allow any tabernacles on the tables used for the Mass. Make the table look like a dinner table. Make it portable, to imply that it is not sacred, but could do double duty for anything, such as a conference table or for playing cards. Later, put at least one chair at this table.

Make the priest sit in this after Communion to signify that he rests after his meal. Never let the priest kneel at Mass, nor genuflect—people don't kneel at meals."

Desecrating the Mass would open the way for the many other abuses planned by the Freemasons in 1962, for instance their plan concerning the reception of Communion: (30) "Get women and laity to give Communion, say that this is the age of the laity. Start giving Communion in the hand like the Protestants, instead of on the tongue. Say that Christ did it this way. Collect some for Satan Masses."

It is for reason that Pope John XXIII on his deathbed requested the Council stopped, saying, "Stop the Council! Stop the Council!" Now he saw the distressing Third Secret unfolding before his eyes. The abomination of Antichrist prophesied through the ages had now broken into his quarters with plans of the second celebration in the works.

The game plan was to turn the priest around so that he says the Mass facing the people with his back to the tabernacle. This was to suggest that the church should turn its back on God and turn to one another instead, which is what we have seen since the Council (human encounter). A shift of focus has ensued where the emphasis today is on the community of man instead of on God.

"The darkness of Satan has entered and spread throughout the Catholic Church even to its summit" —Pope Paul VI, October 13, 1977

The Third Secret

The crisis of faith discussed thus far was predicted by the Blessed Virgin at Fatima in 1917. Before his election to the papacy as Pius XII, Cardinal Pacelli in 1931 prophesied in response to the Third Secret: "The day will come when the civilized world will deny its God, when the Church will doubt as Peter doubted. She will be tempted to believe that man has become God." He said that the Secret of Our Lady at Fatima was:

"A divine warning against the suicide of altering the Faith, in Her liturgy."

Hence we can understand the significance of 1960 as the appointed year for disclosing the Third Secret, since it was only two years later that they would convene the Second Vatican Council, setting into motion an insidious departure from Tradition unmatched in the history of the Church. The Secret concerned this diabolical infiltration of the Vatican which, if released in 1960, would have prevented this spiritual assault that has all but devastated the Faith and left the Holy City half in ruins.

In 1957 Sister Lucy, the eldest of the Fatima seers, told a Father Fuentes in a letter, "The Most Holy Virgin has told me that the devil is about to engage in a decisive battle against the Virgin." This no doubt referred to the fulfillment of the Third Secret that would begin at Vatican II with the subversion of consecrated souls, as well as the suppression of the Secret. Lucy continues: "And as the devil knows what most offends God, and what will make him gain the most souls in the shortest possible time, he does everything to win consecrated souls from God, for in this manner he will succeed in leaving the souls of the faithful defenseless, and so he will lay hold of them more easily." *(Third Secret of Fatima, Bro. Michael of the Holy Trinity, p. 25)*

The Third Secret was actually the third part of a threefold Secret given by the Virgin to the child seers at Fatima on July 13, 1917, the first two parts of which were released by the Church in 1930. However, the third part commonly known as the Third Secret was to remain a secret until 1960, the reason being "it would become clearer at that time." *(Sr. Lucy to Cardinal Ottaviani, May 17, 1955)* Cardinal Oddi, who read the Secret, commented in 1990 that:

"The Blessed Virgin was alerting us against apostasy in the Church."

According to Cardinal Mario Ciappi who read the Third Secret and who was personal papal theologian to Popes John XXIII, Paul VI, John Paul I and John Paul II, the Secret concerned the destruction of the Faith that would be precipitated by the hierarchy. In a personal communication to a professor Baumgartner of Salzburg, he related:

"In the Third Secret it is foretold, among other things, that the great apostasy in the Church will begin at the top."

As we understand, the Secret foretold that the devil would enter the Holy City and capture the ruling body and then use the clergy to set this destructive debacle into motion. Under their staff the Church would proceed down the path of darkness and apostasy under the illusion of progress, fulfilling the scripture, "There shall be a time, when they will not endure sound doctrine." (2 Tim. 4:3)

Those days have come to pass. In 1970 Sister Lucy spoke of a "diabolical orientation" in the Church and said that "the devil has succeeded in bringing in evil (to the Church) under the guise of good and that the blind are beginning to lead others." She even referred to the progressive bishops as "the blind leading the blind" because of their attempts to do away with devotion to the Holy Rosary.

Sister Lucy of Fatima

Hence what we have seen since the Council is the Church in a state of revolt. The fuse of revolution was ignited at the Council (spirit of the Council), and is now building toward that time when we see all-out revolution in the streets of Rome. According to the mystics, Communism will march over Italy and the red flag will fly over the convents until "they shall fall by the edge of the sword; and shall be led away captives." (Luke 21:24)

Yes, the world will soon be awakened to the existence of an angry God, the most devastating part of it being the realization that we as church have forsaken His legacy on earth, that we have cast aside rules and regulations and have gone running after our whims in the name of obedience. The Pharisees of our time will tremble and shake "because they have transgressed the laws, they have changed the ordinance, they have broken the everlasting covenant." (Isaias 24:5)

The Bible speaks of that time in the last days when the horn of Antichrist would rise up against the prince of the Church: "And it took away from him the continual sacrifice, and cast down the place of his sanctuary." (Daniel 8:11) We are witnessing today the Abomination of Desolation wherein the sins of the people have given the evil one great power over the Mass and sanctuary, fulfilling the prophecy: "And strength was given him against the continual sacrifice, because of sins." (Daniel 8:12)

THIS IS NOT TO SAY that the Mass in our time is invalid, but that the liturgy is defective. When we speak of validity, we are not speaking of what is legal or proper, but we're speaking of the reenactment of Christ's Sacrifice that takes place in spite of the priest's actions. The Sacrifice offered through the centuries in the proper rite is the same Sacrifice offered today in the improper rite, so in that sense there is continuity with Tradition. The modern changes themselves do not nullify the Holy Sacrifice, despite their discontinuity with the past.

It's like a tree in someone's yard. If somebody comes along and papers the tree it may insult the household and make fun of the tree, but it certainly doesn't kill the tree. Neither does it give life to the tree. The tree has its own life from the stump in the ground, and unless its essentials are rooted out of the ground, the tree continues to live.

Likewise, the Mass has its own life through its foundation which is Christ, and just because modernists paper the liturgy with their inventions it doesn't kill the supernatural life of the Mass, unless the essentials of Tradition are actually rooted out of the Mass, which of course never happened. The essential wording of Consecration needed for a valid Mass is:

"This is My Body—This is My Blood"

If there is a lesson we learn from The Passion it is that Jesus Christ can take a punch. When they stripped Him of His garments and cloaked Him with a dirty purple rag He didn't drop dead with the first blow, but endured many hours of abuse. Likewise, when modernists stripped Our Lord of His royal, liturgical garments (Tridentine) and cloaked Him with their Novus Ordo rag He didn't just expire, but has continued with us, fulfilling His promise that He would always remain

126

with His Church "even to the consummation of the world." (Matthew 28:20)

As such, faithful Catholics are called to remain with Christ in their parish churches in imitation of St. John and the Blessed Virgin who remained at the foot of the cross amidst the sacrilege. Their example sets the stage for all the true apostles of the last days to remain anchored at the foot of the cross and not flee the cross by leaving their parishes and joining side chapels, for such flight only fosters a timid, underground mentality which is entirely out of character with the Church Militant. Christ today is being profaned in His own House and by His own priests, and we do Him no service by running off and leaving Him hanging there. To win the battle we have to stay in the arena in the spirit of Machabees and his men who went into the temple and restored the true altar. Our encouragement is the knowledge that Christ remains with us in His Church as the invincible foundation that neither principalities nor powers can budge. We have "an immovable Kingdom" (Hebrews 12:28) though the walls of this Kingdom have crumbled in our time.

But when the Third Secret is [20] released in its entirety this will encourage the Church Militant to go forward and build those walls back up to the glory of God. This is the fighting help from Heaven needed to revive the troops and spur them on to victory.

---

20 *Cardinal Ratzinger who assisted in the supposed release of the Third Secret in June, 2000, apparently admitted later that the Vatican release was a cover up. The said release was a well orchestrated attempt on the part of Cardinals Sodano and Bertone to conceal the Third Secret by saying it pertained to things past and not future, and they used Cardinal Ratzinger as their pen in drafting a lengthy commentary aimed at burying the Fatima Secret. According to Bishop Williamson, a priest acquaintance from Austria told him that Cardinal Ratzinger confided (to the Austrian priest) that one of the things weighing heavily on his conscience was his mishandling of the Fatima Third Secret in 2000. Concerning the June 2000 statement Ratzinger reportedly said "my hand was forced."*

But it is also the instrument of Heaven to bring the people to their knees. Father Malachi, who read the Secret, stated in a 1998 radio interview that if the Third Secret were made public the confessionals and churches would be filled with parishioners on their knees. The Secret would shatter this latter day deception that "the long reign of sin has ended" and make us realize that our rejoicing and merry-making since the Council have been the work of the deceiver who "entered into the temple of God."

While at Fatima on May 13, 2010, Pope Benedict XVI went out of his way to set the record straight concerning the Third Secret when he said that it concerns "future realities of the Church which are, little by little, developing and revealing themselves." He said it is about the present "attacks on the Pope and the Church from within the Church" which show "that the greatest persecution of the Church does not come from enemies outside but is born from sin within the Church." The pope also told the crowd of 500,000 pilgrims in the Fatima Piazza:

"He would be deceiving himself, who thinks that the prophetic mission of Fatima is concluded."

Let us pray the good Pope will glorify the truth and release the Third Secret in its entirety, that it may rekindle a love of the Faith and encourage a restoration of the Church back to its former position of honor as it stood before the Second Vatican Council.

Let us only pray it doesn't trigger his assassination, for we will then witness the culmination of this ongoing plan of these last times to put the Faith to death (Third Secret). The growing rumors of assassination reflect a plan afoot against the Holy Father that could very well materialize without prayer, fulfilling the prophecy: *The Mystical Body will be without its head.* Let us pray for the safety of the pope, that the Church may not have to be renewed by his own blood.

WITH ALL THAT HAS transpired since the Council, it's important that we not despair and believe that Christ has abandoned His Church. The present crisis does not mean the Catholic Church has been destroyed or ended, but that it is being attacked. When Christ said that the gates of hell would never prevail against His Church, He in fact was saying that there would be a battle ahead, but He promised to remain in our midst (tabernacle) and fight our battles if we would simply bend a knee and call upon Him.

St. Teresa of Avila said the Catholic Church is Jesus Christ walking through the centuries. Hence, Jesus Christ is again walking the path of Calvary amidst the shouts of modern day high priests who seek to discard the legacy He left us. The Mystical Body is truly passing through its Passion, but Christ calls upon the true apostles of the last days to hold the fort and assist Him in restoring the Church.

For these are the *true* "elements which have suffered injury through accidents of history" that "are now to be restored." The injury wrought by the historic accident of Vatican II is unprecedented and most certainly warrants restoration. And whereas the Council did not intend this statement to mean that pre-Vatican II practice should be restored, it nonetheless can be interpreted this way for the glory of God.

Renewal to Center Around Eucharist

The single greatest means of restoring the Catholic Church is to bring back the Latin Tridentine Mass on a universal scale, though this won't happen overnight because of the great opposition against it that presently exists. As they say, Rome wasn't built in one day so neither will it be rebuilt in one day, but there are positive steps that can be taken in the meantime to build toward that time.

The most important elements of worship to be restored right now are those things that most effectively cause us to adore the King of kings on his throne. All that has been left to us in the way of scripture and liturgy are subservient to the end that we bend our knee to God and keep the Commandments, so a good way of fostering this adoration during these apostate times is to incorporate elements of the old Mass into the Novus Ordo such as the use of Latin and the practice of receiving Communion on the tongue while kneeling.

This would correct the present practice of Communion in the hand which has been a major deterrent in the spiritual advance of the Church. This was introduced to encourage the conciliar idea of a "common priesthood" since it suggests that lay persons may share in this priestly privilege of touching the Host.

However, Benedict XVI does not want the faithful receiving Communion in their hand nor does he want them standing to receive. According to Vatican liturgist Monsignor Guido Marini, the pope is trying to set the stage for the entire church as to the proper norm for receiving Communion, for which reason communicants at his papal Masses are now asked to kneel and receive on the tongue.

"Kneeling highlights the truth of the Real Presence in the Eucharist, helps the devotion of the faithful, and introduces the sense of mystery more easily," Marini told L'Osservatore Romano on June 26, 2008.

This is confirmed by Pope Benedict himself: "We Christians kneel before the Blessed Sacrament because, therein, we know and believe to be the presence of the One True God." (May 22, 2008) The pope offered the following as the single greatest remedy against the New Order of pride which presently predominates in the Church:

"Kneeling in adoration before the Eucharist is the most valid and radical remedy against the idolatries of yesterday and today"—Benedict XVI, May 22, 2008

The pope's initiative is in accord with the Church's 2000 year tradition and is being done in order to foster a renewed love and respect for the Eucharist which presently is being mocked and treated with contempt. The various trends and innovations since the Council (guitar liturgy, altar girls, lay ministers, Communion in the hand) have worked together to destroy our regard for the Eucharist, thus advancing the spiritual death of the Church. After all, the Eucharist is the very life and heartbeat of the Mystical Body around which the entire Church must revolve.

Kneeling coincides then with the Church's centuries old ordinance that only the consecrated hands of a priest touch the Body of Christ in Holy Communion. **"To priests alone has been given power to consecrate and administer to the faithful, the Holy Eucharist."** (Council of Trent) This teaching is beautifully expressed by St. Thomas Aquinas in his Summa Theologica: **"Because out of reverence towards this Sacrament, nothing touches it, but what is consecrated; hence the corporal and the chalice are consecrated, and likewise the priest's hands, for touching this Sacrament."**

It is for reason that Pope Paul VI in his May 1969 pastoral letter to the world's bishops reaffirmed the Church's teaching on the reception of Communion, stating: **"This method on the tongue must be retained."** *(Memoriale Domini)* This came in response to the bishops of Holland who started Communion in the hand in defiance of the centuries old decree from the Council of Rouen (650 A.D.) where this practice was condemned. **"Do not put the Eucharist in the hands of any lay person, but only in their mouths."** To date this age old prohibition has never been legally overturned.

Today Communion in the hand is carried on illicitly as a "common law" practice and has become a major tool of the enemy to destroy the Faith throughout the world. This practice serves no other purpose than to warp our conception of Jesus Christ and to nourish contempt for the sacred mysteries. It is no wonder St. Basil referred to Communion in the hand as **"a grave fault."**

That is to say, Communion in the hand is not tied to Catholic Tradition. This practice was first introduced to the Church by the heretical Arians of the Third Century as a means of expressing their belief that Christ was not divine. Unfortunately, it has served to express the same in our time and has been at the very heart of the present heresy and desecration that is rampant throughout the universal Church. If we have 'abuse' problems today it is because the Sacrament is being abused—it's backfiring on us!

Thanks to Communion in the hand, members of satanic cults are now given easy access to come into the Church and take the Host so that they bring it back to their covens where it is abused and brutalized in the ritualistic Black Mass to satan. They crush the Host under their shoes as a mockery to the living God, and shall we assist it with our casual practice? Among themselves the satanists declare that Communion in the hand is the greatest thing that ever happened to them, and we do nothing to stop it?

Hence the Holy Father is doing his part to try to purge the Church of abuse and we as members of Christ are called upon to assist him. His designs for the reception of Communion are nicely reflected in a statement by Cardinal Canizares Llovera, the prefect for the Vatican's Congregation for Divine Worship and Discipline of the Sacraments, speaking to Life Site News on July 22, 2009: "It is the mission of the Congregation for Divine Worship and Sacraments to work to promote Pope Benedict's emphasis on the traditional practices of liturgy, such as reception of Communion on the tongue while kneeling."

The pope's plan to have the faithful receive in the traditional manner is not a mandate, but bishops and clergy are nonetheless bound to follow his lead. Unfortunately, the practice of kneeling for Communion is discouraged in many dioceses and in some cases is even banned, but the faithful are never bound to honor these directives. Here is where the faithful have that God given right to place their **true moral conscience** forward in a spirit of **true religious liberty** so that they can remain subject to the pope. The directives of the Holy Father are never subject to the scrutiny of the bishops, and pastors with their flock have every right to put his directives into practice for the edification of their communities.

In an interview in December, 2008, Cardinal Llovera spoke concerning the best way to receive the Eucharist: "What does it mean to receive Communion in the mouth? What does it mean to kneel before the Most Holy Sacrament? What does it mean to kneel during the Consecration at Mass? It means adoration, it means recognizing the real Presence of Jesus Christ in the Eucharist; it means respect and an attitude of faith of a man who prostrates before God because he knows that everything comes from Him, and we feel speechless . . . That is why it is not the same to place in the hand, and to receive communion...in a respectful way. It is not the same to receive communion kneeling or standing up, because all these signs indicate a profound meaning."

In short, today's crisis revolves around the Church's failure to recognize the Divine Presence of Jesus Christ in the tabernacle, this being the end fruit of reform. And whereas the single greatest remedy is to universally restore the high altar where Mass is said again facing the tabernacle (ad orientum), the next best thing is to return to our knees before the Holy Eucharist. Without this basic humility before the Blessed Sacrament, our efforts at restoration are vain. The most orthodox thing one can do is to abase himself before God in the Eucharist, without which there is no orthodoxy.

The faithful would do well to consider the conduct of Moses when he approached the burning bush in the mount. The Lord ordered him to put off his sandals because he was on holy ground. And *"Moses hid his face: for he durst not look at God."* (Exodus 3:6) And to think that this was only a manifestation of God's presence, not an actual physical presence.

With how much greater reverence must we approach the altar where the Creator Himself dwells day and night in full Body and Spirit? Shall we mock Him and do a little dance for Him (guitar mass) and then stick our dirty hands out and try to make the Lord of Hosts our pet wafer? God Forbid!!

For those who would approach the Eucharist in a casual, nonchalant manner, let them consider the warning of St. Paul in Holy Scripture:

"Whosoever shall eat this bread, or drink the chalice of the Lord unworthily, shall be guilty of the Body and of the Blood of the Lord. . . For he that eateth and drinketh unworthily, eateth and drinketh judgment to himself, not discerning the Body of the Lord." (1 Corinthians 11:27, 28)

Bibliography

Amerio, Romano, *Iota Inum,* Italy, Ricciardi Publishing House, 1985.

Brother Michael of the Holy Trinity, *The Third Secret of Fatima,* Rockford Illinois, TAN Books and Publishers, 1992.

Carre, Marie, *AA Apostle -The Memoirs of an Anti-Apostle,* Illinois, TAN Books and Publishers, 1991.

Casini, Tito, *Nel Fumo di Satana-Verso t'ultimo scontro,* Florence Italy, April 1976.

Compton, Piers, *The Broken Cross: Hidden Hand in the Vatican,* Australia, Veritas Publications, 1984.

Davies, Michael, *How the Liturgy Fell Apart: The Enigma of Archbishop Bugnini,* Balwyn Vic Australia, AD Books, 2000; *Liturgical Time Bombs in Vatican II: The Destruction of the Catholic Faith Through Changes in Catholic Worship,* Illinois, TAN Books and Publishers, 2003; *Pope John's Council,* Kansas City, Missouri, Angelus Press, 1977.

Gamber, Fr. Klaus, *The Reform of the Roman Liturgy,* Una Voce Press, 1993.

Graber, Dr. Rudolph (Bishop of Regensburg), *Athanasius and the Church in our Time,* Germany, Van Duren Publishing Company, 1974.

Kolberg, Theodore, *Der Betrug des Jahrhunderts (The Deception of the Century),* Germany, November 1977; *Umsterz im Vatikan? (An Overthrow in the Vatican?),* Germany, January 1977.

Lefebvre, Archbishop Marcel, *A Bishop Speaks,* Scotland, Una Voce Press, 1963-1974; *I Accuse the Council,* Missouri, Angelus Press, 2nd Edition 1998; *Open Letter to Confused Catholics,* Missouri, Angelus Press, 1986.

Marsaudon, Yves, *L'Oecumenisme vu par un Franc-Marcon de Tradition,* France, 1965.

Marty, Jean, *Avertissements de l'Au'dela a l'Eglise Contemporaine -- Aveux de l'Eufer,* (Translated from French by Nancy Knowles Smith), France, 1978.

McBride, Ella, *Roses From Heaven,* Orange Texas, Children of Mary, 1988.

Rademacher, Mary, *Our Lady of the Roses Mary Help of Mothers (Blue Book),* Lansing Michigan, Apostles of Our Lady, 1981-1983.

Rynne, Xavier, *The Fourth Session,* London, Herder & Herder, 1966.

Wiltgen, Fr. Ralph, *The Rhine Flows into the Tiber,* Illinois, TAN Books and Publishers, 1967.

Miscellaneous Sources (articles, websites)

Leo J. O'Donovan SJ, *Karl Rahner SJ (1904-84): A Theologian for the Twenty-First Century*

Andrea Tornielli, *Dossie Liturgia Uma Babel Programada,* 1992

Venari, John, *Fr. Karl Rahner-Heresy and Amor,* 2009

Weiskittel, John K, *The Bugnini File: A Study in Ecclesial Subversion*

www.fatima.org
www.insidethevatican.com
www.smwa.org
www.sspxasia.com
www.vatican.va (official source for all Vatican documents quoted)

All scriptural references taken from the Douay Rheims Catholic Bible, 1899 edition

*"It is absurd, and a detestable shame,
that we should suffer those traditions
to be changed which we have
received from the fathers of old"*

—*The Decretals (Dist. xii, 5), cited by St. Thomas
Aquinas in his Summa Theologica, II, I, Q. 97, art. 2*

9581556R00088

Printed in Great Britain
by Amazon.co.uk, Ltd.,
Marston Gate.